AMARNA

City of Akhenaten and Nefertiti

Nefertiti as Pharaoh

AMARNA
City of Akhenaten and Nefertiti

Nefertiti as Pharaoh

JULIA SAMSON

With an Introduction by Professor H. S. Smith

 OXBOW | books
Oxford & Philadelphia

To the Department of Egyptology at University College London,
past and present, with gratitude and affection.

This edition published in the United Kingdom in 2023 by
OXBOW BOOKS
The Old Music Hall, 106–108 Cowley Road, Oxford, OX4 1JE

and in the United States by
OXBOW BOOKS
1950 Lawrence Road, Havertown, PA 19083

© Oxbow Books & Julia Samson 2023

Paperback Edition: ISBN 979-8-88857-026-5
Digital Edition: ISBN 979-8-88857-027-2 (epub)

First published in 1978 by Aris & Phillips Ltd

Oxbow Books is grateful to the Petrie Museum for their collaboration in bringing out these new editions

Printed in England by Micropress, Suffolk.

For a complete list of Oxbow titles, please contact:

UNITED KINGDOM
Oxbow Books
Telephone (0)1226 734350
Email: oxbow@oxbowbooks.com
www.oxbowbooks.com

UNITED STATES OF AMERICA
Oxbow Books
Telephone (610) 853-9131, Fax (610) 853-9146
Email: queries@casemateacademic.com
www.casemateacademic.com/oxbow

Oxbow Books is part of the Casemate Group

Front cover: Modern cast of a bronze weight in the form of a recumbent bull. Original object from Amarna, Egypt,
late Dynasty 18 (*c.* 1352–1327 BC), now in the Egyptian Museum, Cairo. Petrie Museum UC24340.
Image courtesy of the Petrie Museum of Egyptian and Sudanese Archaeology, UCL.

CONTENTS

LIST OF PLATES

Please note that in the reissue of Part I those illustrations originally in colour are now in black and white.

ACKNOWLEDGEMENTS

My gratitude, as unending as his patience has been, goes to Professor H. S. Smith who suggested this book in the first place and who has envisaged and stimulated a series of works on the material in the Museum as a whole. He has been my unfailing mentor throughout, but none of the views expressed in the book should be laid at his door. The project was started under the benign aegis of Professor Emery whose sad loss we all deplore. During the writing of the book I have had unstinting assistance both in this country and abroad for which I want to express my warmest appreciation to all those who have helped.

In particular I wish to thank Dr. Eidden Edwards, Keeper of the Department of Egyptian Antiquities at the British Museum for allowing me to see their store collection, and his assistants for sparing their valuable time. Dr. P. R. S. Moorey, Assistant Keeper of the Department of Antiquities, Ashmolean Museum, Oxford, gave me every facility to work in the Department, handle the Petrie material there and study the store collection for which I am very grateful to him and his helpful staff. My warm appreciation, too, goes to M. Jacques Vandier, Conservateur en chef du Département des Antiquités égyptiennes au Musée du Louvre for his kindness, and the determined help of his assistants who under strike conditions secured for me all the facilities I needed.

I am very grateful to the late Dr. William Stevenson Smith, then Curator of the Department of Egyptian Art, Museum of Fine Arts, Boston, and Dr John D. Cooney, Curator of Egyptian and Classical Art at the Cleveland Museum of Art, for their helpful documentation. Dr. Nicholas Fintzelberg, Chief Curator, San Diego Museum of Man, kindly sent photographs of the 'princess' figures in that collection, which were admirably supplemented by the drawings of my co-operative colleague Miss Joyce Townend, on a visit to the States.

The great majority of the photographs in the book are the result of the time and trouble spent in the College Central Photographic Service for which my very full appreciation goes to Mr. E. Hitchcock and his skilful assistants. To this I add my gratitude to Dr. S. K. Mathews of the Ealing School of Photography, and his willing assistants for the plates they so ably contributed.

For illustrations other than those of objects in the College I want to thank the Griffith Institute, Oxford, for plates 42, 14b and Miss Helen Murray for her promptitude; the Ashmolean Museum for plate 9; the Louvre for plate 5b and Dr. Henri Riad, Director of the Cairo Museum, for allowing the use of the plates of the Cairo fragment of the coregency stela, plate 55c, and those of Tutankhamen's ivory box lid and golden throne, plates 42 and 14b. Thanks for the photographs of the Berlin heads of Nefertiti go to the Staatliche Museen, Berlin. The Egypt Exploration Society has kindly permitted the use of the map (plate A) from *The City of Akhenaten*, Part *II*, and the plan and elevation of the city (plates B and C) from *The City of Akhenaten*, Part *III*. I should like also to thank Miss Ann Petrie who has been exceedingly helpful in arranging access to her father's unpublished Journal from the site.

I am grateful to Dr. Andrée Rosenfeld of the British Museum for her advice on the current nomenclature of the stones used in the Ancient World. In the Petrie Museum my special appreciation for on-the-spot help goes to Dr. David Dixon, Curator, and Mrs. Adams; and in the Department to Dr. Geoffrey Martin for time spent away from his own work on objects from the Amarna royal tomb; to the Secretary of the Department Miss Anthea Page for her absolutely vital initiative; and to Dr. Rosalie David for the vigilant and searching eye she cast over the manuscript. At home my heartfelt thanks go to Alison King for her unfailing encouragement and generous and imaginative help.   1972

ABBREVIATIONS

Acta Or.	Acta Orientalia, University of Copenhagen
AEG and G	Elizabeth Riefstahl, *Ancient Egyptian Glass and and Glazes*, Brooklyn Museum, 1968.
AKK & G	H. Müller, *Ägyptische Kunstwerke, Kleinfunde und Glas*, Berlin, 1964.
ASAE	Annales du Service des Antiquités de l'Egypte., Cairo.
Ashmolean	Ashmolean Museum, Oxford.
ATP	The Akhenaten Temple Project (University of Pennsylvania) Vol I, Warminster, 1977.
B.M.	British Museum, London.
CAH	The Cambridge Ancient History, Cambridge University Press (Vol. 11 - Chapter XIX - 1971).
CdE	Chronique de l'Egypte; Fondation Egyptologique Reine Elisabeth, Brussels.
Cairo	Cairo Egyptian Museum, Cairo.
C/A	*The City of Akhenaten*, part I, T. E. Peet, C. L. Woolley and others, 1923; Part II, H. Frankfort, J. D. S. Pendlebury and H. W. Fairman, 1933; Part III, Vol. I Text, Vol. II plates, J. D. S. Pendlebury, J. Cerny, H. W. Fairman, H. Frankfort, L. Murray Thriepland and J. Samson, 1951. All are published by the E.E.S., London, W.C.1.
CCG	Cairo Catalogue Général.
E.E.S.	Egypt Exploration Society, London, W.C.1.
GM	Göttinger Miszellen, Göttingen, Germany.
JARCE	Journal of the American Research Centre in Egypt, Cambridge, Mass.
J.E.A.	Journal of Egyptian Archaeology, E.E.S., London
JNES	Journal of Near Eastern Studies, Chicago.
MDIK	Mitteilungen Der Deutschen Archäologisches Institut KAIRO.
M.D.O.G.	Mitteilungen der Deutschen Orient Gesellschaft-Berlin, 1911/12; 1912/13; 1913/14; 1917.
MMA	Metropolitan Museum of Art, New York, U.S.A.
PSBA	Proceedings of the Society of Biblical Archaeology 1879 - 1918.
P. Scarabs	W. M. Flinders Petrie, Scarabs and Cylinders with names, London, 1917. Reprinted Warminster 1974.

P.T/A	W. M. Flinders Petrie, *Tell el-Amarna,* London, 1894. Reprinted Warminster 1974.
Rec. de Mons. Egyptienne	J. Capart, Recueil de monuments égyptiens, Brussels, 1905.
RTA	N. de Garis Davies, The Rock Tombs of El Amarna, 6 volumes, 1903, 1905 (2), 1906, 1908 (2), The Egypt Exploration Fund (now Society), London.
Vandier, Manuel d'Archéologie	J. Vandier, Manuel d'Archéologie Egyptienne, III, Paris, 1958.
Z.Ä.S.	Zeitschrift für Ägyptische Sprache, Leipzig.

NB. The spelling Nefernefruaten has been adopted in Part II as opposed to Neferneferuaten in Part I: and the hyphen deleted from the name ANKHESENPAATEN. In the marginal references of Part II one initial precedes the names referred to, save for those who have died, from whose names initials are omitted.

ADDENDA AND CORRIGENDA TO PART I

p. 20, line 15 - for Berlin, read Cairo

p. 21, caption 3 - for Berlin, read Cairo

p. 26, Note UC002 - for Armenienne, read Amarnienne

p. 28, note 10 - for J. F. Harris, *Egyptian Art,* Spring Books, pl. 28, London, 1936, read J. R. Harris, *Egyptian Art,* Spring Books, pl. 28, London, 1966.

p. 29, caption 11 - for H. 11.3 cm., read H. 6 cm

p. 46 note UC037 - for UC 037, read UC 073

p. 56, line 5 - for "Nubian", read pointed.

p. 58, note UC 017 - for UC 017, read UC 071

p. 64, add to caption III - UC 1957

p. 77, note UC 23979 - for UC 23979, read UC 23679

note UC 23689 . . . - for UC 23689, read UC 23680,

p. 88 note UC 1243 . . . - for UC 1243 . . . , read UC 1243, 1241

note UC 23209 - for UC 23209, read UC 23205

note UC 2020 . . . - for UC 2020 . . . , read UC 2020, 23689 and 23601

line 27 - for Asiatic, read woman

p. 90 note UC 1636 . . . - for UC 1636 . . . , read UC 1636, 1183, and 2139

p. 94 note UC 2028 - for UC 2028, read UC 2081

p. 99 note UC 376 - for UC 376, read UC 376A

PREFACE TO THE 2023 EDITION

In the 1970s, a much-anticipated new series of publications illustrated objects and themes related to the excavations of the archaeologist William Matthew Flinders Petrie (1853–1942) in Egypt, and aspects of the collection of University College London's Petrie Museum of Egyptian and Sudanese Archaeology. A young couple setting up in business in the early 1970s, Aris and Phillips published these works, written by members of the UCL Egyptology Department, in their *Modern Egyptology* series. Building on Petrie's own observations, the authors of these volumes aimed to complete the great task of publishing the Petrie Museum of Egyptian and Sudanese Archaeology's vast collection, and to present some of the research that Petrie himself was not able to address in his own published works during his lifetime. As the current Curator of the Petrie Museum, it is a great privilege for me to support Oxbow Books in their mission to republish the series, which remains a key source of information for all those interested in object-based approaches to the study of the ancient world.

The Petrie Museum, part of University College London (UCL), is home to one of the largest and most significant collections of Egyptian and Sudanese archaeology in the world. Free to visit, this extraordinary collection tells stories about the lives of ordinary people who lived along the Nile Valley thousands of years ago. Originally set up as a teaching collection, the Petrie Museum comprises over 80,000 objects housed together with an internationally important archaeological archive. It is a collection of world firsts and 'oldests': the oldest woven garment; the oldest worked iron objects; the first known depiction of loom weaving; the oldest known written document about women's health; the earliest veterinary treatise; the oldest will on paper. The Museum has Designated Status from Arts Council England, meaning that it is considered to have outstanding resonance and national cultural significance. The collection has a substantial, visible international reputation for research, supporting hundreds of researchers every year, both remotely and in person.

The Petrie Museum is named after Flinders Petrie, who was appointed in 1892 as the first Professor of Egyptian Archaeology and Philology in the UK at UCL. Over three-quarters of the material in the Museum comes from excavations directed or funded by Petrie, or from purchases he made for university teaching. In 1880 at the age of 26, Petrie travelled to Egypt to survey the Great Pyramid. For the next five decades he was at the forefront of the development of archaeology in Egypt and later in Palestine, and his detailed methodological approach continues to shape the discipline today.

Petrie worked at more sites, with greater speed, than any modern archaeologist: seeing his life as a mission of rescue archaeology, Petrie aimed to retrieve as much information as possible from sites that were shrinking dramatically in size as Egypt modernised during the late 19th and early 20th centuries. He published a large part, but not all, of the finds from his excavations in his illustrated typological volumes, arranged according to object types and themes. Today, much of the Petrie Museum's collection is displayed and stored in a way which reflects these publications: for example, several storage cupboards are dedicated to the material illustrated in the 'Objects of Daily Use' volume, and objects in the drawers are arranged according to the order of the published plates. This offers a unique opportunity for researchers to engage with Petrie's typological and methodical approach to archaeology, as well as with the history of museum collections.

The first catalogue to be published in the *Modern Egyptology* series was *Amarna: City of Akhenaten and Nefertiti* in 1972 by Julia Samson, Petrie Museum Honorary Research Assistant. As official publishers to the UCL Egyptology Department the series went on to produce facsimile reprints of eight of Flinders Petrie's most important site reports and many of his object catalogues, originally published through the British School of Archaeology in Egypt. The substantial annual royalties from these reprints were paid into the 'Petrie Fund' at the time, which provided special grants to students in financial need.

In many ways, the new reprints of this classic series can be seen as the latest layer in a vast 'publication stratigraphy' of the thousands of finds from Flinders Petrie's excavations, which now live in museum collections around the world. On reading these volumes, I hope that readers will also be inspired to learn more about the Petrie Museum collection and its fascinating history.

Dr Anna Garnett
Petrie Museum of Egyptian and Sudanese Archaeology, University College
London
January 2023

PUBLISHER'S PREFACE

Oxbow Books is pleased to present this title in our *Classics in Egyptology* series. This series of facsimile re-issues is comprised of two sub-series. The first consists of 16 typological catalogues produced by W.M. Flinders Petrie based on his massive collection of Egyptian artefacts. Mostly excavated by Petrie during many seasons of campaign in the last years of the 19th and early decades of the 20th century, they now reside in the Petrie Museum at University College London. Published between 1898 and 1937 and long out of print, the catalogues were re-issued in facsimile by publishers Aris and Phillips in the 1970s. These were followed in the next 15 years or so by publication of a number of newly commissioned titles, based on more recent examination of elements of the Petrie Collection by contemporary experts, under the name *Modern Egyptology*. A selection of these additional titles forms the second component of our own series.

The archaeology of Egypt continues to fascinate. Multi-disciplinary investigation and research continues unabated, encompassing methodologies, scientific and data processing techniques, theoretical approaches, and even whole paradigms that were unheard of in the 1970s and undreamt of when Petrie was working in Egypt. Yet all the titles included in this series continue to be invaluable sources of basic data, providing an unparalleled resource that can easily be cross-referenced with the actual materials they describe and discuss. They remain within the Petrie Collection where they may be accessed and re-examined as new research flourishes. As historic documents, the Petrie catalogues stand as exemplars of the craft of typological classification, the backbone of modern archaeology – much of which, though refined by absolute dating and another 100 years of research, still stands the test of time.

A note on presentation

The facsimile titles of Petrie's catalogues re-issued in the 1970s were produced from scans of the original publications. Scanning technology at that time was not of the standard or resolution of today. The scans are no longer available, nor has it been possible to obtain, and in doing so destroy, original copies of the Petrie catalogues. These titles have therefore, of necessity, been rescanned from the 1970s re-issues. Where necessary the pages have been digitally enhanced for clarity of reading and to ensure the good quality of the plates, though inevitably a few are not of the standard we might wish, because of the quality of the previous scan, and occasional blocks of text are not precisely 'straight' or evenly situated on the page. However, some pages in the 1970s re-issues had been inserted in the wrong order and this has been corrected. The originals were produced at a folio size. The pages have been reduced slightly to standard A4 for ease of shelving and because this has the effect of slightly improving the scanned images. In some cases, illustrations were presented to scale and the original scale is given on the plate. There were also no digital files available for titles included in the *Modern Egyptology* series, so these too have been scanned from printed copies.

INTRODUCTION
by H. S. Smith

The purpose of this book is to illustrate and discuss some Key Pieces from the site of Tell el-Amarna in the Petrie Museum in the Department of Egyptology at University College London. This museum primarily comprises the private collection of Egyptian antiquities excavated and purchased by the late Sir W. M. Flinders Petrie during his long and distinguished archaeological career in Egypt. It was acquired by the College in 1913. To it have been added generous gifts, notably that of the Egyptian Collection of the late Sir Henry Wellcome by his Trustees in 1964. The Petrie Museum is utilised by the Department of Egyptology in its teaching and research, but its collections are made available to outside scholars and students and are open to the public. Petrie himself published a large part, but not all, of his collection. This volume is the first of a number of works designed to complete this great task.

Tell el-Amarna is the modern name of the site of the ancient Egyptian city of Akhetaten, "The Horizon of Aten". It is situated on the east bank in a great bay of hills formed by the cliffs of the eastern desert, near Deir Mowas in Middle Egypt about half-way between Cairo and Luxor. In the middle of the fourteenth century B.C. Pharaoh Akhenaten chose this virgin site to be a new royal residence and capital city of all Egypt, and to be the centre of the state-cult of the sun-god in the form of Aten, "the Sun-disk". The city with its temples, palaces, state buildings and great private mansions was soon built, and Akhenaten moved in with his Queen, Nefertiti and his court. The cult of the sun was the sole official cult in the city, in contrast to the normal Egyptian practice of worshipping many gods under many different forms. Akhenaten, "The Spirit of Aten" and his family were the principal devotees of the cult, in the universality of which Akhenaten came to believe to such an extent that late in his reign he gave orders for the names of all other gods to be chiselled out of temple inscriptions and monuments all over Egypt. This action has caused him to be spoken of by various writers as the world's first monotheist, as a great religious reformer and revolutionary, as the "heretic" Pharaoh, or as an insane religious fanatic. After Akhenaten's death, his successor Tutankhaten fairly soon returned to the traditional capital of Thebes, restored the state cult of Amen-Re and changed his name to Tutankhamen; the cults of Egypt's traditional gods were officially recognised once more. Akhetaten was abandoned. At some time after this, the name of Akhenaten was officially pronounced anathema, and he was referred to as "the fallen one of Akhetaten". The temples he had built to the Aten all over Egypt were razed to the ground, figures and inscriptions of Akhenaten and his god were hammered out on all public monuments, and the city of Akhetaten was demolished and despoiled, never to be re-inhabited.

1

Because of their unusual history, Akhenaten and his city have provoked great public interest during recent years. The material from Tell el-Amarna described in this book is of outstanding artistic and scientific interest, because, with the exception of four pieces from the Wellcome Collection, it was all bought or excavated by Petrie in his pioneer excavation at the site in 1891-92. Unlike much Amarna art purchased on the antiquities market and published in recent years, Petrie's materials have a known and detailed provenance and their authenticity cannot be called into question. Their special importance is that they mostly came from the largest and most impressive building at Amarna, the Great Palace, which was unique in its plan and its lavish polychrome decoration. Though subsequent excavation at Amarna by the Deutsche Orient Gesellschaft before the first war and the Egypt Exploration Society between the wars yielded buildings of great importance, none rivals the Great Palace in its scale nor in the decorative techniques used. In his excavation report, *Tell el-Amarna* (1894), Petrie published many of his finds; the work was remarkable for its time. However, only a proportion of even the finest objects were illustrated, and these in photographs that do them no justice: and his descriptions were summary. In view of the exceptional intrinsic interest of the art of Amarna, and the fact that it is the only ancient Egyptian city which has been at all thoroughly excavated, full publication of Petrie's material is of prime importance.

The author of this work, Mrs. Julia Samson, commenced study of Petrie's Amarna collection under Professor S. R. K. Glanville in 1934, and produced a chapter concerning it in the Egypt Exploration Society's publication *City of Akhenaten,* Vol. III. She returned to the Egyptology Department at University College in 1966 as an Honorary Research Associate. She has done me the honour of asking me to contribute to her book a sketch of the historical background to the discoveries at Tell el-Amarna for those readers unfamiliar with ancient Egyptian history. Many interesting works, both learned and speculative, have been written in recent years about the exceptional problems which Amarna history raises. The summary that follows attempts only to present what is reasonably well established, without argument or discussion of evidence.

HISTORY

The reign of Akhenaten's father, Amenophis III (*c.* 1405-1368 B.C.) was peaceful and prosperous. Egypt's client states in Palestine and Syria, which had been brought under her sway by the conqueror Tuthmosis III in the mid-fifteenth century, though they might intrigue against one another, were serving Egypt's interests under the watchful eyes of Egyptian legates. A temporary balance of power between Egypt, the Hurrian state of Mitanni, the Hittites, the Assyrians and the Babylonians had been achieved by judicious use of Egypt's gold, by diplomacy and dynastic marriages. Never had imported luxuries from the Levant and the Aegean world flowed into Egypt in more profusion. In the south Egypt had secured her frontier beyond the Fourth Cataract, and Amenophis was building great Egyptian temple cities along the fertile Dongola bend to create a new province. In Egypt itself, Amenophis had built for himself and his Great Royal Wife Ty a splendid palace at Malkata in western Thebes (opposite modern Luxor) in which to celebrate their jubilees, and an enormous mortuary temple beside it. Temples were founded, restored and extended both at Thebes, the capital, and throughout the country. The endowments for these were munificent, more especially for the great temple at Karnak at Thebes, the seat of the state god Amen-Re. Full temple treasuries and granaries in Egypt meant not only the ability to withstand bad Nile years and the long summer droughts, but the capacity to bring new land under cultivation and to stimulate craftsmanship and artistic production. Priests and state officials were richly rewarded for their services by the King, and were able to build for themselves fine town-houses and villas, with large estates to support them. Our sources tell us little of the common people, but they can hardly have failed to benefit in some ways from the stable economic and agricultural conditions, and the availability of work on state projects during the barren months of the year.

At this time, though the ancient cults of Egypt's gods flourished and prospered in their cities and their priesthoods had become virtually a professional body, yet the state cult of Amen-Re had been endowed with so large a proportion of Egypt's agricultural land and received such large annual imposts from the Pharaoh's dependencies in the north and south that its position was paramount, and it functioned as an arm of the state executive. Amen was the patron god of the Theban XVIIIth Dynasty to which Amenophis belonged. During the fifteenth century, his cult became ever more fused with that of the sun-god Re, whose foremost cult city was at On (Heliopolis), north of modern Cairo and near the great administrative and military capital at Memphis. The sun-god was the lord of the universe, the creator of gods and mankind, and the giver of all life and its benefits. The king ruled this world according to Re's divine plans by virtue of being his son. During the reigns of Amenophis III's grandfather Amenophis II and his father Tuthmosis IV, an ever-increasing number of hymns and prayers to the sun-god as the giver of life were composed and inscribed on stelae, tomb-doors, and other monuments. Though the sun-god is addressed in his Heliopolitan form of Re-Harakhty (Horus of the Horizons), he is occasionally referred to in these hymns as Aten, the disk of the sun. The growth of sun cult has been plausibly attributed in part to the results of contact with the religions of the Levant after Tuthmosis III's conquests, but this cannot be proved; we should know more if Heliopolis had been excavated.

An Egyptian crown prince in the XVIIIth Dynasty was sometimes married to the eldest daughter of the reigning king and his chief Queen. But Amenophis III made Ty, daughter of the priest Yuya and his wife Tuyu, neither of whom apparently were of royal stock, his Great Royal Wife. Ty's name, unlike that of earlier queens, is regularly placed in a cartouche and included in royal titularies; and

3

she is represented as of equivalent stature with the King — sure marks that she held exceptional power and influence. Prince Amenhotep (Akhenaten's birth name) was born of this union. Of his early years there is virtually no record; presumably he was brought up by a tutor in the royal residences at Thebes and elsewhere, being educated in court ritual, the arts of government, warfare and the royal sports. Before he ascended the throne he was married to Nefertiti, whose parentage is unknown; on the basis of her name, which means "the beautiful one who is come" it has been suggested that she may have been the Mitannian princess Tadukhipa; but this is unsupported by evidence, and would have been quite contrary to Egyptian royal practice.

Prince Amenhotep probably acceded to the throne about 1368 B.C., and took the names Neferkheprure Waenre Amenhotep, that is, he became Amenophis IV. Within two or three years however he had changed his last name to Akhenaten and adopted the worship of Aten. At the beginning of his reign he presumably resided mainly at Thebes; there he built very large temple buildings to the Aten in the precincts of the Karnak temple of Amen-Re. As these buildings were completely dismantled after Akhenaten's death and the blocks of which they were composed were used to fill pylons, it is uncertain whether Akhenaten attempted to convert the whole existing temple to the worship of the Aten, or whether he simply added shrines to the Aten to it. The work however shows the royal family worshipping the Aten disk, in the new, informal style adopted for official art at Amarna. Several famous tombs at Thebes belonging to officials of his father also received additions carved in this style.

In the sixth year of his reign, Akhenaten beat the bounds of his chosen new capital city, and ordered the carving of the great rock-stelae that mark its confines. These include not only the city on the east bank but a large area of agricultural terrain on the west bank opposite. The stela proclamation runs: "As my father the Aten lives, I will make Akhetaten for the Aten my father in this place. I will not make him Akhetaten south of it, north of it, west of it or east of it. And Akhetaten extends from the southern stela as far as the northern stela, measured between stela and stela on the eastern mountain, likewise from the south-west stela to the north-west stela on the western mountain of Akhetaten. And the area within these four stelae is Akhetaten itself; it belongs to Aten my father; mountains, deserts, meadows, islands, high ground and low ground, land, water, villages, men, beasts and all things which the Aten my father shall bring into existence eternally forever. I will not neglect this oath which I have made to the Aten my father eternally for ever." He visited Amarna again in year 8, while the city was being built, and added to the stelae; it would seem that it was in year 8 that Akhenaten, Nefertiti and their daughters finally installed themselves at Amarna.

A passage in the boundary stelae, formerly interpreted to mean that Akhenaten swore never to leave his city, refers to his not extending the boundaries of the city itself.

The whole interpretation of the events of these early years of

Akhenaten's reign depends upon whether Amenophis III was still alive in year 9 of Akhenaten or whether he had died before Akhenaten acceded. Akhenaten endowed the Aten with a royal titulary, which he slightly changed in or about year 9. A number of inscriptions from Amarna and elsewhere have been shown to associate the royal names of Amenophis III and Akhenaten with the later form of the Aten titulary, and there exist scenes in which Amenophis III is shown, apparently alive, with the later Aten names. There are also various wine dockets and business documents which suggest, though they hardly prove, that year 1 of Akhenaten followed close upon year 27 of Amenophis III; yet the last year of Amenophis III was his 38th. There is thus inferential evidence for assuming a coregency between father and son, though some favour a length of nine, some of twelve years. This would mean that all during the period of the foundation of Amarna and the early years of Akhenaten's residence there, Egypt was really being ruled by the senior King, Amenophis III, from Thebes. Amenophis III would thus have continued to rule a state of which the official cult was that of Amen-Re, while allowing his younger co-regent to build a new capital city for the cult of Aten and even to build monuments of the Aten at Karnak itself. This cannot be regarded as impossible, but conflicts oddly with what we know of the practice of the Pharaonic office; until a document dated by both kings is discovered which proves the long co-regency, it seems best to preserve an open mind. A letter from the King of Mitanni, Dušratta, which promises the same friendship to Akhenaten as he had observed with Akhenaten's dead father, Amenophis III, would settle the matter were the date of its docket fully preserved; but there is a lacuna before the extant figure 2, which means that the original may have read year 2 or year 12.

The life of the royal family at Amarna is most fully depicted in the reliefs on the walls of the rock tombs that the great state officials carved for themselves in the cliffs, though fascinating and delicate fragments of large frescoes from the royal palaces are also preserved. In the tombs the Pharaoh is shown with Nefertiti and his daughters in the Window of Appearances of the Royal Palace, bestowing honours and largesse on his bowing and obsequious high officials; again with his family, driving in his chariot between the temple of the Aten and the Palace along the Royal Way, escorted by his guard and applauded by the crowd; worshipping in the temple; or dining and drinking in the privacy of the palace. In all these scenes Nefertiti is shown as of equivalent stature to the King, and her names Neferneferuaten Nefertiti are enclosed in a cartouche; evidently she enjoyed a greater influence at court than Queen Ty did. Even in official scenes, the King and Queen are shown hand in hand; the scenes of them banqueting in the palaces are depicted with a wealth of intimate detail not normally recorded in Egyptian art.

The royal pair had six daughters, Meritaten, Maketaten, Ankhesenpaaten, Neferneferuaten the younger, Neferneferure and Setepenre, all of whom were born before year 9. Famous scenes in the tomb of Huy, the Chief Steward of the Royal Household of Queen Ty, record a visit of Queen Ty to Amarna some time before year 12 with her daughter Baketaten. A lintel in the tomb represents Amenophis III with Ty and Baketaten on one side, and Akhenaten, Nefertiti and four daughters on the other; some supporters of the co-regency believe this shows that Amenophis III himself visited Amarna very near to the end of his reign. A jubilee held for the King and the Aten in year 12 and a festival in which foreign tribute was ceremonially offered at a specially erected pavilion in the same year, mark for some scholars the beginning of Akhenaten's sole rule.

In all the scenes showing the King and his family, the disk of the sun is shown above them, extending its rays towards them; these rays end in hands, which sometimes hold the Egyptian symbol of life to the noses of the King and Queen. This favour is granted to them alone; where officials are shown in the doorways of their tombs reciting the famous hymns to the Aten, the god itself is not portrayed. Alone among Egyptian gods the Aten is given a royal titulary and celebrates periodical jubilees; significantly these are concurrent with the jubilees of the King. It is the King and Queen who are the chief actors in the cult of the Aten; their colossal statues surrounded the open courts of the temples, which apparently contained no images of the gods, although the walls were probably covered with scenes of the worship of Aten. The god was physically present in his disk above and the cult seems mainly to have consisted in dedicating offering-libations, incense and oblations to open altars. The Aten communicated directly to the King, and it was the King alone who interpreted the divine will. In the longer hymn to the Aten, which has been thought to have been composed by the King himself, a long poetic passage ascribes the creation of all the phenomena of the universe to the Aten, and asserts that all creatures move and have their being only by virtue of the sun's rising and infusing life into them each morning. The final section runs:—

"Thou art in my heart, there is none that knows thee but thy son Neferkheperure Waenre, and thou hast made him wise through thy plans and thy omnipotence. The world exists by thy hand, as thou hast made them. When thou arisest, they live; when thou settest, they die. Thou art thyself the span of life, by thee do men live. Eyes can see beauty until thou settest; but when thou settest on the right all work is set aside. When thou risest, thou makest (all things?) to prosper for the King; (the power) of motion is in every leg (only) because thou hast founded the earth. Thou hast raised them up for thy son, who came forth from thy flesh, the King of Upper and Lower Egypt, who lives in Truth, the Lord of the Two Lands, Neferkheperure Waenre, the Son of the Re who lives in Truth, Lord of Diadems, Akhenaten, may he live long, and for the Great Royal Wife, his beloved, the Mistress of the Two Lands, Neferneferuaten Nefertiti, may she live and grow young for ever and ever."

While this hymn is certainly monotheistic in the sense that all creation and all power is ascribed exclusively to one sole being, yet the theocratic element is clear; the Aten rules only through his son Pharaoh Akhenaten, who is almost in the situation of the god's incarnation on earth. In this light it is not difficult to picture the motives for Akhenaten's persecution of all other gods in the later years of his reign.

The Queen's name Neferneferuaten Nefertiti is often placed in twin cartouches as if to resemble a Pharaoh's titulary. Akhenaten at the end of his reign had a coregent, whose *prenomen* was Ankhkheprure-beloved-of-Neferkheprure (or Waenre) and whose *nomen* was Neferneferuaten-beloved-of-Akhenaten (or Waenre). A regnal year 3 appears with this titulary in a *graffito* in the tomb of Pere at Thebes. This coregent later changed these titles to Ankhkheprure as *prenomen* and Smenkhkare as *nomen,* presumably on becoming sole Pharaoh at the time of Akhenaten's death, which wine dockets suggest happened in his seventeenth year of reign. Since Petrie's time, this successor to Akhenaten has usually been regarded as a young male of uncertain parentage, possibly a brother to Tutankhaten. The eldest daughter of Akhenaten and Nefertiti has been thought to have become this successor's King's Great Wife, since her name Meritaten appears, in a cartouche, with various forms of Ankhkheprure's titulary on two objects. Queen Nefertiti has been considered by some to have died, disappeared or been disgraced during Akhenaten's reign, since at the pleasure palace of Maruaten at Amarna a Queen's cartouches were replaced by those of Meritaten; but the displaced cartouches have now been shown to be those of the King's Wife Kiya, a lesser consort of Akhenaten's. However, eight examples of the *prenomen* of the coregent have now been identified which show the female termination *.t.* Reconsideration of a usurped Pharaonic representation from the tomb of Tutankhamen suggests that it depicts a female Pharaoh. None of the figures thought to represent a male coregent of Akhenaten's can be positively proved to do so, nor can it be shown that Meritaten's title King's Great Wife was related to a male coregent or successor. If then Ankhkheprure was a female, she may have been either Nefertiti herself or Meritaten. Nefertiti fits the changes in titulary, particularly the fact that the coregent retained her name Neferneferuaten, and other evidence better; Mrs. Samson sets out the arguments in detail in Part II of this book.

If Akhenaten was buried in the sarcophagus prepared for him in the royal tomb dug in a desert valley 4 km. east of Amarna, where his second daughter Maketaten had been buried, his corpse did not survive the deliberate despoliation of the tomb. On the sarcophagus fragments, it is Nefertiti who is shown tending Akhenaten; so presumably she survived him. Probably it was she who invited the Hittite king Suppililiumas by letter to send a son to marry her and become the King of Egypt, and so prevent her having to marry a commoner. Suppililiumas, understandably, delayed to discover the true situation, and the son, when sent, failed to reach Egypt. The Pharaoh Smenkhkare, whether Nefertiti or not, cannot have reigned long, and was succeeded by Nebkheprure Tutankhaten. Who his parents were is uncertain; but he must have come of the XVIIIth Dynasty royal line because he calls Amenophis III 'father' and a lock of Ty's hair was in his grave. Unless there was a long coregency between Amenophis III and Akhenaten, he cannot have been Amenophis III's son, but he may have been Akhenaten's by a minor Queen. Akhenaten and Nefertiti's third daughter, Ankhesenpaaten, became his King's Great Wife. The young king soon left Amarna for Thebes, where his name was changed to Tutankhamen and his Queen's to Ankhesenamen. The officials and courtiers followed, leaving their Amarna houses sealed. The state resumed its former course, and the names of Amen and other gods were restored on the monuments, though the systematic destruction of Akhenaten's monuments may belong to the time of Horemheb and the XIXth Dynasty. Tutankhamen was buried at an age of under 20 in his famous tomb at Thebes, after a reign of nine years, by Ay, who succeeded him. Ay's priestly title 'god's father', sometimes held by the fathers-in-law of kings, was included in his *nomen,* and may have constituted his claim to the throne. Some believe he married Ankhesenamen, Tutankhamen's widow. After four years of reign, he was succeeded by the general Horemheb, who was not of the XVIIIth Dynasty royal house, though his King's Great Wife, Mutnodjmet, may have been Nefertiti's sister. His reign marks the beginning of a new era.

The traditional judgement on Akhenaten has been that, however great the spiritual value of his religious thought and the aesthetic worth of the artistic trends he encouraged, his reign was a political disaster, in that his inaction lost Egypt the allegiance of its Levantine client kingdoms. But this view appears to be incorrect, and was based on an interpretation of the Amarna letters, the archive of cuneiform tablets found in the Records Office at Amarna. These comprise much of the diplomatic correspondence of the courts of both Amenophis III and Akhenaten with the rulers of the great states of the Near East, and with their own client kings. The older view over-emphasised the reliability of the complaints of King Rib-Addi of Byblos to the Egyptian court. Throughout this correspondence, Rib-Addi constantly asks for military reinforcements, and protests that his enemies, Abdi-Ashirta and his son Aziru of Amurru are ruining the whole structure of Egyptian power in the Levant; he does not baulk at accusing Pharaoh's own Egyptian officers of conniving with his enemies. In point of fact, it is clear that Abdi-Ashirta and Aziru, no less than Rib-Addi, were client kings of Egypt, in correspondence with and to some extent trusted by the Egyptian court. Aziru's presence in Egypt was demanded by Akhenaten, and eventually, after many delays which he explained by the proximity of the Hittites, he obediently came to the Egyptian court. It is true that after Akhenaten's death, Aziru did ally himself with the Hittites against Egypt for motives of personal and local advantage. It is therefore quite probable that Rib-Addi was right that Aziru was playing a double game; but this was the game that all the Levantine and Syrian dynasts played, probably including Rib-Addi himself. The Egyptian court's concern was to see that no major disadvantageous balance occurred between the great powers in the Near East and that the intrigues and combinations of the client states and independent cities were controlled at a level where they did not threaten Egyptian commercial interests or precipitate major conflicts. For this reason, minor rivalries between Egyptian client states and flirtations with enemy powers were tolerated, so long as they were supervised by Egyptian legates and correctives could be applied as needed in the shape of military force or financial support. The Amarna letters, read as a whole, make it clear that this policy was carried out on the whole successfully throughout Akhenaten's reign, and that despite intense rivalries, local wars and mutual accusations, Egypt's influence in Syria and the Levant was little weaker at the end of the reign than the beginning. In the south a campaign was actually undertaken in Akhenaten's name to suppress Beduin who were attacking the gold mines of Wadi El-Allaqi in Nubia, and he continued his father's policy of temple building and town foundation in the Dongola bend.

The history of Akhenaten's reign must therefore be judged more on the results of his internal policy. His Egyptian successors pronounced a firm and enduring judgement against it; whether on dynastic or religious grounds or both, his name was pronounced anathema and his monuments, so far as possible, razed from human memory. Most modern writers, while admitting that his regime was in the event a political failure, have admired the King's determination to "rule in sincerity", and have applauded the spirit of Akhenaten's faith and art.

THE SITE

The stelae set in the cliffs by Akhenaten in years 6-8 define the area of the city of Akhetaten on the east bank of the Nile and its agricultural territory on the west. The eastern cliffs enclose a bay of flat desert six miles long from north to south and three miles deep. From the bay a large desert *wadi* leads through the eastern hills: up *Plate A* a side *wadi* four miles from its entrance is the ruined royal tomb. Either side of this *wadi* in the cliffs are two groups of rock rombs excavated for the nobles of Akhenaten's court. Some of these were unfinished at the time the city was abandoned, and it is not certain that any received the burial for which it was intended, as they were deliberately ruined. But the reliefs of these tombs, splendidly recorded by N. de G Davies early in this century, are our chief source for the reconstruction of the appearance of the city of Akhetaten, and the life which Akhenaten and his court led there. These scenes are all in the new artistic style favoured by Akhenaten, which discards the formality of traditional Egyptian official art; they have one special value, namely that they contain detailed depictions of many of the buildings of the city. Though these are often difficult to interpret because of the Egyptian technique of combining plans and sections, and because the official buildings of the city have been razed in most cases to their foundations, yet many have been identified and their value may be assessed from the splendid reconstructions of the city published by the Egypt Exploration Society expedition.

The city itself did not fill the whole bay, but lay along the river. Its nucleus, the "Central City", comprised the main public buildings and *Plan Plate B*

SKETCH MAP SHOWING
THE SITE OF AKHETATEN
ON THE EAST BANK
AND THE APPROXIMATE
EXTENT OF EXCAVATIONS
(BRITISH & GERMAN)
UP TO FEBRUARY, 1932

Modern Villages
  "   "   Cultivation
High Nile
Unexcavated Ruins.
Excavated   "   "

Scale of Miles & Kilometres.

A. Tell el-Amarna

Plate C. Lower, right corner

was probably built first. The river quays appear to have opened directly on to the "Great Palace", which comprises three separate constructions. The first, the "State Apartments", is a stone building of vast proportions, partly lost under the cultivation. Probably it was entered from the north through a gateway leading on to a huge court surrounded with colossal statues of the King and Queen. A pillared portico on the south led into a transverse pillared hall and thence to a rectangular court. Beyond lay a series of three logitudinal pillared halls, which may have been throne rooms or audience chambers; they were flanked by colonnaded courts. Though it is clear that this building must have been used for the most impressive state ceremonies at Akhetaten, its exact status is unclear, as its plan is unique and few of its features have been identified in tomb representations. Beyond the audience chambers on the south lay an enormous hall built of mud brick with a forest of square pillars: this was evidently built hastily and rapidly rather late in the history of the city, and may have been Smenkhkare's coronation hall. The third element of the "Great Palace" consists of the Royal Harem, the servants'

10

quarters and magazines. These lie in a long narrow range of mud-brick buildings to the east of the state apartments along the length of the "Royal Road", Akhetaten's chief thoroughfare. The harems contained columned halls and courts, their pavements and walls delightfully painted and tiled with scenes of pools, plants, birds, fish and animal life; decorative rectangular pools were surrounded by loggias and private chambers.

A main ceremonial way led from the river through the internal courts of the State Apartments and the harems to a three-arched bridge over the Royal Road into the "King's House", where Akhenaten, Nefertiti and their daughters lived their private family life. It was possibly on this bridge that the King's main "Window of Appearances" was situated: here there would have been a splendid view along this wide processional avenue and room for the crowds witnessing royal ceremonies. The "King's House" was not dissimilar in plan from the normal high official's villa, but was grander, and was surrounded by a spacious garden. On the south of the "King's House" was the "Records Office", where in 1887 the cuneiform diplomatic

11

C. *Reconstruction of the centre of the city.*

Plate C. At the top

archive known as the "Amarna Letters" was found. To the east again were quarters for the entertainment of foreign embassies and notabilities, and beyond on the desert edge, the barracks of the military and police.

From the "King's House" it was a chariot ride of less than a quarter of a mile northwards along the "Royal Road" to the "Great Temple of the Aten", past large ranges of temple magazines. The temple enclosure forms a great rectangle on an east-west axis, entered through a pylon from the "Royal Road". A second pylon gave access to a hypostyle hall, called "The House of Rejoicing of the Aten". Along a processional way punctuated by gateways lay a series of six rectangular courts, called the "Gem-Aten", also filled with offering tables for oblations to the Sun's Disk. The central part of the enclosure was empty, but at its eastern end lay a sanctuary consisting of a pylon with porticoes and beyond a series of courts containing a great altar and offering tables. The pavilion where foreign tribute was received in year 12 lay abreast of the northern enclosure wall, while the high priest Panehsy's house lay outside the south-east corner of the enclosure.

To the south and north of the central buildings lay the main living areas of the city. The high officers of the Court evidently had the first

12

choice of sites at Amarna, and in general sited their villas near to the Central City, in the main on the axis of the royal road. These villas consist basically of a courtyard, garden, garden shrine, porch, one or two open loggias, a main columnar entertaining room, a private hall, master bedroom, lavatory, bathroom, harem and extra bedrooms: a stairway led to the roof, while in the courtyard at the back were grain storage bins, ovens and other service facilities. Gaily painted decoration was often present in the main hall. Round these large villas, there congregated the houses of all the retainers of the great official, often built *pêle-mêle* and in haste regardless of the axes of the streets. The houses of the middle class in general formed orderly blocks in the South City and the North Suburb, where the quarter nearest the Aten Temple was occupied by corn merchants. The "Royal Road" progressed through the North Suburb to the North Palace, apparently a place of diversion, beautifully decorated, with fish ponds, aviaries and decorated mangers for several species of mammals. Beyond was the North City, surrounded by a great brick fortification wall, over the gate to which was probably another "Window of Appearances". Within was another large palace, which on rather fragile evidence has been considered to have been assigned to Queen Nefertiti after her alleged "disgrace". Round this palace were great houses, which however had no domestic quarters, and may therefore have served as the official residences of the Vizier, Treasurer and other great dignitaries of state. At the extreme north end of the bay was a substantial building, perhaps a customs house, while at the southern end, separated from the city, was a royal pleasure pavilion known as the Maruaten. Industrial sites were scattered, but on the whole, like the glass works and sculptors' workshops, were not far from the "Great Palace".

Such was the city of Akhetaten. Hastily built and casually planned parts of it certainly were: yet as the restorations in the Egypt Exploration Society's reports vividly demonstrate, its central quarters were of great dignity and architectural harmony. As the material described in this work shows, this was matched by decorative ingenuity, delicacy and taste: the effect on any embassy arriving from a foreign land must have been one of overwhelming beauty. Owing to the hazards of excavation in the Nile Valley, Tell el-Amarna is the only great ancient Egyptian city of which any major proportion has been dug; and this may well remain so. It is also the only city from which all the finds can be exactly dated to a short period of twenty years. Publication of evidence upon which its evaluation depends is therefore vital, and Mrs. Samson's book is devoted to this end.

THE SIGNIFICANCE OF THE COLLECTION
by the author

Perhaps the significance of this Collection from Amarna was best discerned by Jean Capart, the eminent Belgian egyptologist, who described it to me as the greatest teaching collection in the world. The clue to this achievement can be found in Petrie's own words from the site where, in his day-to-day Journal he wrote of the glass he was finding "I keep every scrap to show the colours and patterns of this age". This approach of his led to the formation of a collection within which it is possible again and again to find the parallel or cite the example needed to make a point in the explanation of the Amarna civilisation. In it there is evidence on some of the questions which have puzzled egyptologists and the material covers a wide field of information about Akhenaten's city, Akhetaten, now called Amarna. The great majority of the objects are from Petrie's excavation of the central city in 1891-92, particularly in and around the Great Palace and the Great Temple, and further south. This gives a homogeneity to the finds, and where a piece can be assigned to a part of one of these vast edifices it can indicate developments which occurred as the building progressed. Other objects were bought by Petrie; some have been acquired direct from the excavations on the site by the Egypt Exploration Society between the years 1921-1937, and others from these digs came with the gift to the Museum from the Wellcome Trustees in 1964.

Chronologically the Collection spans the whole of the Amarna period, from the scarab on which Akhenaten is still named Amenophis (IV), to the stela where he is shown with his co-regent. Historically it includes the sealing stamp which is very possibly a relic of Queen Ty's visit to Amarna in year 12, as well as the little gold figure from Qurneh that indicates the presence of the youngest Amarna princesses at the Court of Tutankhamen when he returned to Thebes.

Plates 51a/b

Plate 52
Plate IV

The fragments of the stela are published in their present form for the first time. They have been pieced together over the years since as a student of Professor Glanville, I began finding them in the Museum and interpreting them. It was then that I visited the Egypt Exploration Society's dig at Amarna, directed by J. D. S. Pendlebury, and he asked me to include some objects from this Collection with his finds from the site in "City of Akhenaten III". This led to Professor Fairman discerning that a fragment of limestone in Cairo found by Pendlebury in 1934 belonged to the Petrie Stela. Since then more fragments have been joined together, and the name of Ankhesenpaaten discerned.

In the trio, the young Akhenaten and Nefertiti with, probably,

14

their eldest daughter and heiress Meritaten as a child, are shown as a normal family, not as the stylised impersonal royalty of the past. The Queen wears the typical Theban wig and not, as in the later pair statue of the King and Queen in the Louvre, her tall crown by which Plate 5b the world now knows her. The carving of the apron on the King's *shendyt* kilt is unfinished and by comparisons, explains the unfinished state of the King's one nude colossal statue from Karnak about which for years there has been so much supposition, including the theory that he was not able to father his six daughters. In these statuettes he is shown without the exaggeration that occurred when the art form changed from the monumental Egyptian style to expressionism.

On a fragment of diorite a young princess is shown with the gross Plate 26 caricaturing of that early period. She has the ovoid head with which the princesses are shown when young, although the old theory that all six had deformed heads is no longer credible. Some possibly inherited the dolicocephalic-shaped head, but as adults they are shown normally like Ankhesenamen is on Tutankhamen's furniture. On a Plates 14b, 42 band from a column in the central palace which, on architectural and stylistic grounds can be judged as later than the diorite relief, the Plate 27 softening of the lines in the princess's portrait can be seen.

This mellowing of the art is evident too, in the contrasts between Nefertiti's portraits from the early years when the city was being Plate 18 built and the sketch of her in her later years wearing the tall crown. Plate 19 Akhenaten's profile, although only partial, also records the move Plate 23 towards naturalism. The small, unfinished head of Nefertiti, in the Plate 2 round, immortalises a stage in the carving of a masterpiece and is remarkable in its likeness to the painted limestone head in Berlin and Plate 4 the unfinished example. Plate 3

Innovations are visible in the scenes of daily life at Amarna. The relief of two offering bearers enables comparison between the way Plate 28 ordinary people are presented at Amarna and in similar scenes from the preceding reign in Thebes. In place of the exquisitely carved, elegant, stiffly posed stock figures of a procession in the tomb of Ramose, these two young temple attendants are individuals. Forging ahead as they do in eager movement with their offerings, the relief is an example of the use of space in a composition and the use of angles to urge a design forward. The second figure, slightly smaller, which gives a degree of perspective to the design, is carrying a stack of bouquet "cones" about the use of which queries have been expressed. When compared with those on the raised border of the stela on plate 55a, it seems likely that these are flower holders for an upright stand.

The unfinished figure from the tomb of Ay records the participa- Plate 29 tion of a humble onlooker in an Amarna scene, apart from being a lamentable reminder of the thieving of works of art from the site in the last century. In the painted relief of the food carrier another vitalising Amarna influence is evident in the way the design breaks through the rigid lines of the registers to enliven a scene; and vitality is not limited to the larger and more important works in the city. It is evident on the ring bezels and seals where foreign parallels, which became a factor in the Empire of the XVIIIth Dynasty, are noticeable. The movement of animals in this small art echoes the love of nature shown in the wall and floor painting of the palaces.

From the thousands of pieces of glazed and inlaid tiles which Petrie brought back, with hundreds of the moulds in which they were made, the faience industry can be seen as an integral part of Amarna art and architecture. It must have assumed almost the proportions of the building itself, for the remains of glazed decorations abound, from walls, doors, columns, and possibly floors, from composite statues, composite inlaid portraits on the walls, inlays on the furniture and from inscriptions, besides the multiplicity of the faience small art that was worn and used in daily life. The varied fragments from the central city are proof of the intricacy of detail lavished on the faience objects of which but a small selection are included in this book. The colour sense of the designers is shown in such examples as the red tiles inlaid with green leaves, white and yellow lotuses and buds, forming garlands against a red ground. The sophisticated use of colour perspective is evident in the warm colour over a colder hue on the tile of a duck which must be one of the earliest examples of such finesse in the art history of the world. The recognition of the effectiveness of mosaic patterns can also be seen in faience examples.

Plates VI, VIII

Plate VII

Plate VI

Faience inlays in the Collection include squares, circles, rhomboids, all the geometric shapes which studded the capitals of the palm-shaped columns in the palace. There are curved, glazed "ropes" from cartouches, rods from the Aten's rays and pieces of red and blue glazed disks of the Aten which Petrie notes were as large as fifteen centimetres in diameter. Fruits, flowers, fish and lotuses from pond scenes and marsh reeds from around them; foreigners, figures of gods and offerings for the Aten, all spell the variety of the inlaid scenes. If these splendours, like the fragments of faience vases and vessels, jewellery, bowls and kohl tubes with royal names on them, which Petrie found around the palace, were confined to it and the larger houses, the faience *minutiae* were not, since the beads and amulets were found by Woolley as far afield as the houses of the workmen in their Eastern Desert Village and must have been for the whole population. These merit a book to themselves. The numerous and varied amulets are a record of the degree of inspiration and courage of Akhenaten's endeavour to establish a universal monotheism at this period of world history, and, in a country so entrenched in the worship and fear of hundreds of animal and anthropomorphic gods and goddesses. They also record the freedom allowed in the city built and dedicated to the sole worship of the Aten. Amongst the amulets are also some of the Aten symbols.

There is ample evidence in the Collection of the multiplicity of scenes dedicated to the Aten. Some reliefs evince the religious emphasis and the stimulated understanding of the artists in their purpose of expressing the King's beliefs. The sculptors were faced on unprecedented scale with the challenge of carving scenes of religious and royal significance to be seen in the direct light of the sun. The

Aten ceremonies on the walls and stelae of the roofless temples and courts had to convey their message at all times of the day, at different heights and with the changing emphasis from cast shadows. How successfully the challenge was met could only be known if any of the carvings in the city had remained *in situ*. But evidence of the way the sculptors worked is clear from many pieces in the Collection. They varied the cutting angles and the depth of line and combined the different techniques of sunk-relief (*en creux*) and raised reliefs (*en bas*) in the one subject, sometimes supplementing the emphasis with colour, according to the material and methods used. Two relevant examples are the libation offerings, where the variation would focus the attention of the viewer on the devotional activity in all angles of light from the sun. Similarly, the Queen's profile on the alabaster balustrade which, leading to one of the raised doors in the palace would largely be seen above the heads of the people on floor level, is in the same genre as her portrait on the marble fragment, but the two carvings are given different emphasis of line and depth.

Plates 24, 25

Plate 20

Plate 18

The understanding of a third dimension is evident in the placing of Aten rays behind a head and, in the relief of the offering bearers, by size as mentioned above, as well as by placing the bouquet behind the head of the man on the left. Some of the stone inlay portraits show the same awareness and at least one has rounded-edge carving, to remain above the surface of the wall and cast a shadow. Others are intended to be sunk into the wall flush with the surface. In the best of these the planes of the face are carved so that a play of light would achieve what a tonal painter does by varying hue and tone. The carving of the head of a negro for inlay is bolder but not without modelling on the face; it shows the non-royal inlay, without preparation for the addition of features and regalia which created the composite royal inlays in the style of composite statues. There are pieces of varying sizes in the Collection from such composite statues, the finest being the superbly carved life sized red jasper ankle and heel which would have been joined at the top surface by the gown of the wearer, possibly in limestone or alabaster, just as the king and queen's robes drop to their ankles on the back of Tutankhamen's golden throne. Besides carvings of part of a face in this red jasper, there are other pieces from composite statues including a heavy carving of part of a full sized wig in basalt, curved pieces of blue faience from the King's war crown and a small faience slightly curved crown of Nefertiti's, probably from a statuette.

Plate 24

Plate 28

Plate 38

Plate 40

Plate 41

Plate II

Plate 14b
(UC 112)
(UC 076)
(UC 24274)
(UC 24270)

The naturalistic female statuettes found in the palace and central city would seem to be from groups of the Queen and her daughters. They echo the form of the earlier statues of the King and Queen with their oldest daughters at the base of some of the Boundary Stelae and more information would undoubtedly be obtained if all the examples of these so called "princess" figures, in widely scattered museums, could be considered together. The apparently careless placing of a right hand on the left side of the sandstone "princess" figure is a very unusual example of a pre-Homeric nod amongst the Amarna sculptors of statues, although in reliefs even royal figures

Plates 8a-11

Plate 10

are sometimes given two left or right hands. There is an instance of this occurring on the owner of the stela, despite the rigorous training evident in the studies of hands.

The technically high level reached by the stone carvers can be seen in detail in such signs from inscriptions.* Even on the stamps for clay sealings with the inscriptions of many horses and Queen Ty's name, the carving is competent and would have produced a bold design in the clay, in *bas relief,* as on the first and outermost door of Tutankhamen's tomb. This detailed skill is particularly evident in the carving of the stone inlays where, against the smooth surface the masons gave the fine white limestone, the multi-coloured red and black granite and diorite inscriptions were inlaid and must have been visible, even legible from a distance. Cornices of black granite uraei were inlaid in yellow quartzite, white alabaster was inlaid in red granite, and other combinations used. The competence in carving the brittle stones is consummate. In the smaller inscriptions glass was used for the slim lines of which one limestone piece in the Collection is a fine example.

The glass makers were also artists: the unique fragment of the two young princesses, early in the history of moulded glass, shows most of the techniques of the craft and at the same time, the artistry of the pose portrays their sensibility. Another fine example is the head for inlay, possibly another portrait of a princess. Nothing remains of the delicate inlaid furniture from Amarna which must be imagined from pieces like these. Only on Tutankhamen's furniture is there the possibility of a parallel. The frail gold figure from Qurneh, probably an Amarna princess living at his Court, is possibly from something belonging to him.

No pottery is included in this book and it is anticipated that a study of Mycenaean sherds from Amarna will be published later.

Life at Amarna was cultured; the philosophy advanced for its time; the state unwarlike; the daily life dedicated; nature was appreciated and humour evident. It was a background against which artists could, and did develop. Two unofficial masterpieces in the Collection which testify to their enjoyment are the alabaster "swimming" girl from the perfume holder, and the sketch of a baboon, possibly brushed in on the limestone during an idle moment, and remaining as a tribute to the mastery of the Ancient Egyptian draughtsman.

Plate 55(b)
Plate 35

*Plates 36, 44 and 53
Plate 52

Plate 44

(UC 190)

Plate V

Plate 45 (ii)

Plates 42, 43 and IV

Plate 12a and 12b

Plate 37

18

PART I

Statues and Statuettes

HEAD OF AKHENATEN

This ushabti head of Akhenaten from his tomb was bought by Petrie and exhibited in London on his return from Amarna in 1892. Wearing the *Khat* or "bag" wig with the pigtail at the back, and the uraeus and beard, it resembles a number of other ushabtis from the tomb, particularly one in Brooklyn.[1] But the finely boned features have an unusual delicacy and are strikingly like those of Queen Ty in the schist head from Sinai.[2] The face also resembles Tutankhamen in his statue as Khonsu from Karnak,[3] and his portrait in the Theban trio with Amen and Mut.[4] The eyebrows, nose and full, slightly drooping lips are clearly defined, but the eyes are suggested in a way that gives the face the dreaminess of a contemplative, evident in other remarkable portraits of the King.

[UC 007]
Provenance: Amarna, Royal Tomb. Syenite. Height 7·0 cm. Width 6·0 cm. Lit. W. M. F. Petrie, *Catalogue of Antiquities from Amarna*, 1892, p. 5. J. Samson, *C/A III*, Text, p. 225, pl. CV(12). Comparisons: [1]Brooklyn, No. 33.53(3); [2]Cairo 38257; [3]Cairo 38488; [4]G. Legrain, C.C.G., I, pl. LXII, No. 42.097.

1. Head of Akhenaten showing family resemblance to Tutankhamen. (H. 7 cm.).

HEAD OF NEFERTITI

The arresting similarity of this small unfinished head to the famous painted limestone head of the Queen in Berlin,[1] and to the lesser known unfinished head also found by the Germans in the studio of the sculptor Thutmose,[2] points to the same provenance for this carving, perhaps even the same master hand for it also bears the mark of genius. It has already been given the meditative repose of Amarna royal portraits described by M. Vandier as "*le mystère d'une vie intérieure intense*".

The poise of the Queen's head on her long neck is characteristic. Her distinctive cheekline is suggested, her long eyelid and the straight nose. Her full sensuous mouth, so sharply defined in the Berlin portraits is beginning to be shaped and when finished would have completed the profile of her mature years. On her head is the roughly hewn peg for the addition of her upright crown in another material. The shaping of the ear and the treatment of the stone are at an earlier stage than on the unfinished Berlin portrait.

[UC 010]
Provenance: Amarna (possibly studio of Thutmose). Red sandstone. Height 6·5 cm. Width 6·0 cm. Lit. J. Samson, *C/A III*, text p. 225, pl. *CV* (11). Comparisons: [1]*Cat. Ägyptisches Museum*, Berlin, Inv. No. 21300; [2]*M.D.O.G.* 52, pl. 5.

2. *Head of Nefertiti with preparation for tall crown to be added in another material.* (H. 6·5 cm.).

20

3. *Unfinished Head of Nefertiti (Berlin).*
(H. 36 cm.).

4. *Painted limestone head of Nefertiti*
(Berlin). (H. 50 cm.).

ROYAL TRIO

The unfinished limestone statuette of Akhenaten, Nefertiti and a young princess is important as a record of the early period at Amarna, and for the comparison it affords with other carvings and later developments.

The small triad is cut from a single block of limestone. The King and Queen, backed by a plinth, step forward on a rectangular platform base, while the princess lags childlike on the right of her mother. Her head and the top of the Queen's wig were freed from the plinth which apparently continued behind the taller head of the King, presumably planned to wear a crown.

His clavicles are carved with undue prominence considering his fleshy torso and thighs, with the disproportion evident in early Amarna attempts to show the royal figures realistically. But his figure here, fleshy like his father's in his later years when the artistic realism began, is more that of an oriental monarch than a body distorted by disease. The apron of his *shendyt* kilt has been shaped, but the carving of the kilt not started and this unfinished work is useful for comparison as described below. The King's hand is missing from his left arm which hangs close to his side, while his right arm stretches towards the Queen as they clasp hands in the manner of their pair statue in the Louvre, discussed later,[1] and like the model hands found in Thutmose's studio.[2]

Nefertiti stands with her left foot forward like the King, in the active pose more usual in other periods for a man, rather than his wife. Both wear sandals. The Queen has the taut, upright body of a young woman and wears

[UC 004]

Provenance: A sculptor's studio near the south end of Amarna. Limestone. Height 13·5 cm. Width 11·0 cm. [1]Louvre No. E.15593; [2]M.D.O.G. No. 50, fig. 25; [3]M.D.O.G. No. 52, fig. 25; [4]Cairo, 55938; [5]Cairo, 49528. Lit. [6]P. T/A., p. 31, Pl. I(1); [7]J. Capart, *Rec. de monuments égyptiens,* II, Pl. LXXV, Brussels, 1905.

the Theban wig, not her later Amarna variety, with the lappets hanging from it to her breasts. Between the lappets an oblique line is incised possibly marking the top edge of her gown. Below each breast is an echoing upward curving line, probably to be smoothed away eventually. Her navel is but a rounded depression, in contrast to the triangular shape with a line through it more usual in later years, and at the base of her abdomen are two upward curving lines. Her knees and legs are blocked in somewhat "woodenly".

5a. Royal trio—unfinished limestone statuette of Akhenaten, Nefertiti and a princess. (H. 13·5 cm.).

Plate 8a*

To the right of the Queen and turning slightly away is the small figure of a princess, possibly Meritaten, towards whom her mother holds out her right arm which swings behind her to catch the child's left hand. The left upper arm of the princess remains, stretching out along a ridge similar to that on the left of the figure. The princess has been given her mother's figure in miniature in the manner used by the artists during the early years of the new art when the children are merely small adults, but there is no suggestion of clothing as on her parents, so she may have been planned to remain naked and shoeless in the informal manner sometimes used for the young princesses at Amarna. Her left foot is forward in the emancipated pose. Her right arm, now missing, appears to have hung down close beside her body. The statuette is without an inscription.

22

For similarities and contrasts, the group is useful to compare with the later limestone dyad of the King and Queen in the Louvre. This is on the same scale, but finished, painted and inscribed. In both statuettes, the royal figures are hand-in-hand and stepping forward on a shallow platform base away from a back plinth. In the Louvre pair, Akhenaten, wearing the blue crown, steps forward with a resolute air; Nefertiti is wearing the tall crown introduced during the Amarna years, and her figure has the suggestion of the droop which is more pronounced in the ageing figure of her standing statuette from the Thutmose studio.[3] The Aten names on the back of the Louvre plinth are in the late form prevalent after year 9, and the couple are unattended by a princess, the eldest of whom by then would have been entering her teens.

6. Diagram of finished colossus of Akhenaten (Cairo).

5b. Akhenaten and Nefertiti (Louvre). (H. 23 cm.).

On the dyad, the apron of the King's *shendyt* kilt is carved as it has been started in the trio, and comparison shows the actual method used for carving the kilt, which settles the long controversy as to how it could have been added to the King's nude statue from Karnak. The belt is made by cutting back the surface of the abdomen to leave a ridge, and the linen folds of the kilt are then carved over the hips, curving up to the belt buckle. On the one unfinished colossal statue of Akhenaten found in Karnak, the only one that is nude[4], his kilt would have been added in this way, because the stone is already recessed around the Aten plaques at the waist and would have been further cut back, as on the finished colossus, to make the ridge of the belt.[5] There would have been no necessity for further delineation of the King's figure, about which there has been so much conjecture, any more than on the two

7. Diagram of unfinished colossus of Akhenaten (Cairo).

23

statuettes. This underlines the fallibility of theories about his physical build and condition being based on unfinished statues. Rather than the son of the sun choosing to be represented as unable to father his children, the probability is that the one nude, unfinished statue was never raised to a standing position. It is unlikely that the Amen priests left in Thebes after the royal removal to Akhetaten would have exerted every effort to finish the Aten temple, and if Nefertiti's daughters were the children of someone else and not Akhenaten, it is inexplicable why a son was not introduced into the royal household as an heir.

Petrie found the trio at a "sculptor's place . . . near the south end of the town",[6] presumably Thutmose's. Both he and Capart[7] thought it may have been a model for larger works, possibly like those beneath the Boundary Stelae to which it has resemblances as described on page 28, but it may have been intended as a finished, coloured limestone statuette like the Louvre dyad.

As it stands, it is a record of the royal family, possibly soon after their arrival at Amarna, with the Queen's youthful figure and Theban styled wig, the child princess, and her parents in a protective normal rôle.

NEFERTITI OR A 'PRINCESS' FIGURE

Although known as "The Amarna Princess" for well over half a century, recent comparisons of it with other "princess" figures discovered since its acquisition, and with figures of Nefertiti, suggest that this is not a figure of a princess but a portrait of the Queen.

Plate 8a

[UC 002]
Provenance: Amarna. Reddish quartzite. Height 15·3 cm. Width 8·0 cm. Width at top of broken back plinth 5·5 cm.; at bottom 7·5 cm. Width of chiselled surface right of the figure at thigh level: 8·0 cm. Comparisons: [1]Louvre, W.25409, C. Desroches-Noblecourt, *L'Ancienne Égypte*, L'Extraordinaire Aventure Arménienne, Paris, 1960. [2]Ashmolean Museum, Oxford, 1893-1-41 (260);

In reddish brown quartzite, the upright torso stands gracefully against a plinth. The body is rounded to behind the hips and on the left of the figure was another feature, now grossly destroyed. The head, which was evidently carved in one piece with the body, is broken from the base of the neck, of which the roughened horizontal circle remains. In front of this is the lower edge of the clavicles. Both legs are missing from above the knees, but the right thigh is carved in advance from a stance of one foot forward. The carving of the front of the torso is unspoilt and the figure has a flesh-like reality from the fine burnish of the stone. The smoothed surface of the upright shoulders continues over to the top of the broken back plinth. The breasts are youthfully small and firm in contrast to the abdomen and full hips which are those of a *multiperae* rather than a young girl. There is a horizontal line through the navel as on other examples of such nude torsos from Amarna and on the draped figure in the Louvre, thought to be the Queen.[1]

The broken surface of the back plinth on which no trace of burnish or inscription remains, now slopes obliquely down from the shoulders, and outwards to whatever feature stood at the far end of the ridge, left of the figure. The left arm swings back to meet this at hand level, probably to reach a small following princess whose arm stretched forward along the slightly downward slope of the ridge to meet her mother's hand. The once rounded arm of the main figure is chipped on the top surface, but still finely burnished at the back, as the stone is above and below the ridge.

24

8a. *Nefertiti or a princess figure with left arm swung back like the Queen's right arm in the trio plate 5a.* (H. 15·3 cm.).

8b. *Side view showing ridge as from princess's arm on plate 5a. (H. 15·3 cm.).*

The right arm of the figure is missing. It was freed from the stone at the elbow and the forearm could have reached forward to meet the hand of another in a group. Below the roughened surface where the upper arm was joined, the stone is finely burnished. But although the surface at right angles to this is squared, it is roughly finished with the chisel marks remaining, unlike the other surfaces of the block and as though planned to flank another figure or object.

Plate 9 This links the figure with a named one of the Queen in Oxford[2] and differentiates them both from so-called "princess" figures, some of which have the remains of a princess's name or title. A number of these were also clearly part of a group and all are headless with the legs mostly broken near the knees or at the top. In most it can be seen that one leg was in advance of the other; in a number one arm hung down by the side and in some one arm is bent across the body at the waist, but these poses of the legs and arms were not always carved uniformly on the left or right side and appear as though varied to balance the composition of the figures in a group. In contrast to these poses the statuette described here resembles figures of the Queen with one arm stretched towards a princess as in the trio above and in the treatment of a Boundary Stela statue described below. The stone of the Oxford figure of the Queen is savagely broken but is carved in the same way as these other statuettes and, considered with the figure here, and "princess" figures, suggests that a number of these came from more than one group of Nefertiti with her daughters.

Comparison of these nude statuettes shows the use of and even probably the grouping of different stones in the Amarna tradition. Of the three in this Collection, two are quartzite and one sandstone. In Brooklyn, apart from a larger figure of Maketaten in quartzite,[3] there is one in granite found by Pendlebury in the Broad Hall of the central palace.[4] Another found by him in the same area is of sandstone;[5] two in San Diego are in sandstone, one of Meritaten, found by him in the palace,[6] and another with the fragmentary designation "born of";[7] one in Berlin is of sandstone.[8] The figure of Nefertiti in Oxford is of quartzite. Without seeing and handling all the above examples a full comparison is not possible.

Plates 8a, 10, and 11

The arguments in detail for the largest figure in this Collection being Nefertiti and not a princess are as follows:—

1 Like the Oxford figure of the Queen, this has one side squared but unfinished as though to stand beside another. Both these figures have been carved from quartzite with a dark streak running through it and in both this has been used down the right side of the figure to enhance its roundness. Such attentive selection of the stone and skilled use of it suggests special care given in the same studio to portraits of the Queen.

[3]Brooklyn, 16.46; [4]J. D. S. Pendlebury, C/A III, No. 237, p. 67, pl. LXIX (2); [5]J. D. S. Pendlebury, op. cit., No. 260, p. 68, pl. LXIX (2); [6]J. D. S. Pendlebury, op. cit., No. 261, p. 68, pl. LXIX (2); [7]San Diego Museum, 15298; [8]H. Schäfer, ZÄS, 52, p. 82, pl. 17, Leipzig, 1915.

9. Part of figure of Nefertiti (Ashmolean Museum). (H. 21 cm.).

[9]N. de G. Davies, *RTA*, V, pl. XLI, XLIII. [10]J. Capart, *Lectures on Egyptian Art*, p. 26, fig. 19, University of North Carolina, 1928, and O.U.P. H. Schäfer, *Amarna in Religion und Kunst*, D.O.G. Berlin, pl. 23, 1931. Burlington Fine Arts Club, *Illustrated Cat. of Ancient Egyptian Art*, p. IX, 1930. J. F. Harris, *Egyptian Art*, Spring Books, pl. 28, London, 1936. J. Samson, *C/A III*, p. 226, pl. CVI. J. Vandier, *La Statuaire Égyptienne*, pl. CXI, (5), Paris, 1958.

2 The left arm of this figure swings back to meet the ridge like Nefertiti's arm in the trio above, where her hand clasps the hand of the following princess. This also echoes the technique used on the right side of the Queen's statue below Boundary Stela A where a ridge links the arm of the princess with her mother's figure.[9]

3 The right arm of this example was freed from the elbow and could have reached towards another as the Queen does to the King in the trio above and in other groups.

4 This figure has neither an arm crossing the body nor hanging by its side, both attributes of named figures of the princesses.

The hacking out of names and the almost uniform destruction of these statuettes across the thinner parts of the figures, while leaving the bulk of the stone as found in the palace, points to the aim of the damage being to obliterate the royal portrait rather than to plunder the stone. Had these figures been only of princesses, the attacks may have been less purposeful. If a figure of the King had been included in such groups, its handleable size would undoubtedly have resulted in its total destruction.

Over 40 years ago, Jean Capart, noting that Petrie bought this figure, wrote that he believed it may have come from the studio of Thutmose and he added that he had "hard work to convince one of the most celebrated classical archaeologists that this piece of work was dated seven centuries before the first efforts of the Greeks in statuary."[10]

It is hindsight and the knowledge of "princess" figures excavated since then that enables the present assessment of this as a portrait of the Queen, and not of an Amarna Princess as it has always been described in the past.

FRAGMENT OF A 'PRINCESS' FIGURE

[UC 24324] (W)
Provenance: Broad Hall, Central Palace, Amarna. Sandstone. Height 11·3 cm. Central front width 5·5 cm. Back width 7 cm. Length of arm and hand 5 cm. Lit. *C/A III*, excavation report, p. 66, No. 37, otherwise unpublished. Comparison pl. 55.

Although lacking the fine finish of the stonework on the more fully preserved quartzite torso this sandstone fragment is from a figure in the same *genre*. It was found by Pendlebury in the Broad Hall of the Central Palace at Amarna, with others discussed more generally above. The lower left side of the abdomen remains; the curve of the break left of its centre is made from the line across the navel which is usual in these figures. The pubic fullness is also a typical feature. Part of the upper left thigh remains and a fraction of the right leg showing it was advanced. Left of the figure is a hand and wrist, carved as though it were a right hand. The back of it rests against the thigh with thumb in front and palm and fingers outwards, not possible in a left hand nor in a position which the right hand of this figure could be. It could be the right hand of an adjacent figure, which would be unlike other examples of these group figures with this feature remaining; or it could be a hand carved in a reversed position, which although not unusual in Amarna reliefs where incorrectly placed hands occur in numerous places, is an unexpected carelessness in a carving in the round. Other examples on these figures are in the correct position. The hand rests against a piece of dressed stone, at right angles to the figure and sloping slightly backwards.

See, for example, Plate 55

28

The figure is broken in the middle from front to back nearly at a right angle to the front. The back is completely broken leaving a nearly flat broken surface.

10. Left thigh, and a hand on a "princess" figure. The fraction of right leg is shown slightly forward. (H. 11·3 cm.).

11. Fragment of "princess" figure with back plinth, similar to others from groups. (H. 11·3 cm.).

FRAGMENT OF A 'PRINCESS' FIGURE

This fragment of a nude torso from the original Petrie Collection is of red quartzite. It is broken almost horizontally across the middle and unevenly across the thighs, leaving from waist to thigh on the right side of the body and only the lower abdomen on its left. Although so fragmentary, it is comparable in style with other "princess" figures from Amarna, with the up-curving line in the pubic area. The navel is without the horizontal line through it that these figures usually show.

A protuberance of rough stone down the left side of the figure could have been its arm and hand. The buttocks are rounded and carved on both sides to meet a narrow projecting plinth at the centre back. Although once of dressed stone, the left side of the plinth is completely beaten away and the right side grossly damaged, but on this there are faint signs of shapes which might once have been parts of hieroglyphs.

[UC 082]
Provenance: Amarna. Red quartzite. Height 6·0 cm. Width 8·0 cm. Width of body across top break 6·0 cm. Width of plinth: 2·3 cm. Diameter 8·0 cm. Unpublished.

29

12a. *"Swimming" girl with mortise between the shoulders for her head which would look towards the perfume container that would be held in her outstretched hands. (L. 8·3 cm.).*

FIGURE FROM A PERFUME HOLDER

This young girl's figure is part of a toilet spoon of the familiar XVIIIth Dynasty shape where a girl lies prone with her head raised and her arms outstretched in front of her to hold a perfume container. There is a rounded mortise between her shoulders where her neck would have fitted, with her head carved to look forward to the perfume dish in her hands.

12b. Upright view of the alabaster figure which held a perfume or unguent container. (L. 8·3 cm.).

[UC006]
Provenance: Amarna. Alabaster. Length 8·5 cm. Width 3·5 cm. Lit. J. Samson, *C/A III*, p. 227, pl. CVI (2 and 6).

Despite the missing head, arms and lower legs, the shapely breasts and the flowing lines of her body suggest the flexibility of youth, and the curve of the back with the tautly stretched muscles each side of the waist give the pose a sense of action and show the artist's understanding of anatomy.

Sometimes described as "swimming girls" these figures were carved in wood and ivory as well as stone and although the craftsmanship is usually high, some are stylised and rigid. This figure has the sensitivity of a master-piece, like the royal portraits of the later Amarna period.

BUST FROM A ROYAL STATUE

This quartzite bust from a half life-sized seated royal statue is carved in the finest tradition of the sculptor's technique in hard stone. It is from a composite statue, and the neck is mortised with a clear-cut central rectangle, 6·7 centimetres from front to back, to take the head.

31

Provenance: Amarna. Red quartzite.
Height 20·0 cm. Frontal width 17·0 cm.
Width of left shoulder to centre
back 10·0 cm. Lit. W. M. F. Petrie,
History of Egypt II, p. 224, London,
1899. J. Samson, *C/A III*, p. 226,
pl. CV (9). Comparison: W. C. Hayes,
Scepter of Egypt, II, p. 285, fig. 173,
N.Y., 1968.

*13a. Front view of royal statue bust
showing a mortise for the head, and
wearing a collar-necklace with Aten
plaques of which there are faience examples
in the Collection. (H. 20 cm.).*

*13b. Side view of royal statue bust showing
wrinkles above the waist suggesting a
sitting pose. (H. 20 cm.).*

The damage the bust has suffered appears to have been purposeful. Besides the loss of the right arm, the left is broken from above the elbow and the stone below the waist of the figure has apparently been beaten away. The right breast has been reduced by abrasion, and the left one flattened; this has removed part of the Aten plaques on the left of the necklace and the central pair above the waist. All the plaques contain the early name of the Aten; the top of a cartouche remains on the left arm.

The shapely body has wrinkles both sides above the waist, suggesting plumpness in a sitting figure, but the clavicles and the hollows between them are well defined and the back is curved between the *scapulae* into a slight hollow, where streamers as from a crown are incised. Pleats of the gown are carved over the left shoulder to fall downwards across the body into the long robe so often worn by Nefertiti and occasionally by Akhenaten. As in the similar limestone bust of the Queen in the Metropolitan Museum, New York, the robe is carved over the breast! The carving of the pleats remains at the sides above the waist and, under the left arm, the line of the ribbed or beaded edge can be seen as it is carried on into the knot at the waist in front, where the sash is lightly incised.

The beads of the necklace are carved singly, in detail. Four rows are defined of the usual lotus petal, mandrake and date shapes, with intervening cylinder beads. The Aten plaques are evidently threaded into the necklace and resemble glazed examples in the Collection.

There is no suggestion of a plinth. The carving at the back is lighter and less detailed, perhaps because it was intended to stand against or near a wall. The torso suggests it was a portrait of the Queen, but there is no designation.

MOUTH AND CHIN FROM A COLOSSAL STATUE

This lower part of a face from a quartzite statue is approximately twice life size. The break across the chin, which is almost a clean cut as though damaged from one heavy blow, is 9 centimetres wide and 8 centimetres from

14. Lips and chin from one of Akhenaten's colossal statues at Amarna. (H. 14 cm.).

33

top to bottom. The finished surface of the stone remains on the right side of the broken chin and on the left of the face, along the jaw line to the diagonal break. In his unpublished day-to-day excavation notes from Amarna, Petrie recorded shortly after his arrival that he found in the Palace ruins the lower part of a face of a colossus of Khuanaten [*sic*]. No piece in the Collection other than this corresponds to the description. Pendlebury, from his findings, wrote that the Broad Hall was completely surrounded by colossal statues of the King and Queen, which he estimated were slightly under twice life-size. The Queen's were apparently of sandstone; those of the King of both granite and sandstone.

The fine but not high burnish of the pale red quartzite and the sensitively carved planes of the face give a flesh-like effect. The lips are full and everted; they appear relaxed, despite the fact that—except where they meet on the left side of the face—they are chipped. The curving line where the lips close, and the rise in the cheek by the diagonal break, suggest a faint smile. The chin and jaw line could have terminated in the shape of Akhenaten's prominent chin but would not appear to lead to a pendulous feature.

The life-like carving of the features has an animation, in contrast to the finely carved but immobile majesty of the colossal smiling head of Amenhotep III in the British Museum. This, although stylised in its facial planes, foreshadows the changes which occurred in the Amarna style of carving.'

Facsimile of Plate II. See p. 64.

RED JASPER ANKLE AND HEEL

This life-sized red jasper ankle, heel and section of a foot is realistically observed. With a transverse polished surface across the leg where the white gown would reach it, and another sloping across the instep for the front of the foot to be added, it is clearly part of a composite statue; Petrie noted it in his unpublished excavation journal as the largest such piece he remembered.

The ankle bone is strongly but delicately carved and the fibula shaped as though rising from it. At the back the Achilles tendon is shown with detailed planes. The sole of the foot is shaped with a flat base and a ridge round the edge. Above this, up the side of the foot, is a gentle swelling as though from the weight of the body on it. The jasper of the foot has grey streaks in it and is more yellow than the stone at the ankle and above it, which is an orange to red colour. The photograph can only suggest the genius with which the bones, muscles and tendons have been carved. The finish of this glass-like stone has been described as scarcely short of miraculous.

A small, highly polished, curved but uncut piece of darker red jasper in the Collection (UC 111), and a similar piece with part of a mouth carved on it (UC 112) could have come from the same statue. On the latter the lips remain from the centre nearly to the right corner and below them, the highly polished stone is recessed before the beginning of the outward turn towards the chin. Above the lips the surface has broken away, leaving unfinished jasper, as at the back of the fragment.

14b. *Back of Tutankhamen's golden throne* (Cairo). (Photo: Griffith Institute)

A LION'S HEAD

This small stone head of a lion is sensitively but boldly carved with a characteristically leonine mask. The eyes are carved in detail with convex eyeballs; the nose shaped, and the whiskers incised. Over the head the hair or mane is stylised into a cap-like covering with a central point on the forehead.

35

15. *Lion's head shaped to be fixed into a right-angle. (H. 5 cm.).*

[UC 24278] (W)
Provenance: Amarna, S.W. Quarter, N. Suburb (30/240). Painted pumice stone. Length 8·0 cm. Width 6·0 cm. Height 5·0 cm. Unpublished, except for excavation note, J. D. S. Pendlebury, *C/A II*, p. 87 (T.36.57).

The ears are shaped low down on the sides of the head, and the only remains of paint (red) occurs below and behind them.

The muzzle is carved underneath as though to be fitted or slotted onto a horizontal surface, and the back of the head is a smooth vertical plane, which would fit against an upright. The head would have fitted into a corner at the end of the arm of a chair or throne, where it would have made a comfortable hand rest. It is worn smooth on top and, if the paint once covered the head, this too has worn away, perhaps from the contact of a hand. It is reminiscent of the use of lions' heads on thrones and royal chairs from the Old Kingdom onwards. An XVIIIth Dynasty instance on Tutankhamen's golden throne, is in the corner made by the top of the leg and the upright of the arm.

Notes on Monkey Statuettes

MONKEY STATUETTES AND RELIEFS

In a series of 23 unpublished, coloured limestone statuettes of monkeys found by Petrie at Amarna, and two more from the Wellcome Trust, the animals are shown playing the harp, practising acrobatics, eating and drinking, cosseting their young and driving a chariot. Pendlebury believed that some he found were more than a satire on human behaviour and more than just toys, and were in fact caricatures of the royal family at Amarna.[1] A few in the Collection also suggest the enjoyment of them may have been on two levels, as the pranks of monkeys and, as parodies of the current human scenes. The carving of the small pieces, although careless, is in no way amateur, and sculptors of the repetitive scenes in innumerable reliefs may have enjoyed satirising the unusually informal representations of the royal family—the King, for instance, driving his own carriage with the Queen in it, in unprecedented manner.[2] The statuettes have the vitality of Amarna scenes, earlier toys[3] and New Kingdom papyri.[4]

Most of the figures have the remains of paint on them, which, in some, gives a realistic effect. A number combine relief carving with rounded figures; they are heavy and clumsy. Many stand on their own base but some have an upward-curving base and will not stand alone. A number of groups have a hole or holes through them near the base, and, in such examples as the chariot, if a stick were passed through the hole and a wheel added at each end of it, the "toy" could simulate the mobility of the original.

As the statuettes and the reliefs on them are carved both sides, they have been photographed with a mirror reflection.

Comparisons: [1]J. D. S. Pendlebury, *C/A II*, p. 99, pl. XXXI; [2]N. de G. Davies, *RTA*, IV, pl. XX; [3]Monkeys, Old Kingdom, B.M. 11888; MMA, W. C. Hayes, *Scepter of Egypt*, II, p. 314, N.Y., 1968; [4]B. M. Papyrus, No. 10016.

TWO MONKEY STATUETTES

The Chariot Driver

On both sides of this painted sunk relief, a monkey is shown driving a horse-drawn chariot, from the same end of the block. The stone on this edge and the top and bottom is smoothed. The block was evidently rectangular as the diagonal break down the middle leaves only the haunch, hind legs and tail of the horse, whose body and head were presumably shown on the missing front fragment.

On the obverse, the bony head and prognathous jaw of the monkey is roughly carved but unmistakably simian. It faces left and its thin body is upright in the chariot. Although the arms are carelessly carved, their action

Plate 16

[UC 029]
Provenance: Amarna. Painted limestone. Height 8·5 cm. Width 8·0 cm. Depth 2·0 cm. Unpublished.

37

is vigorous, the right uplifted, perhaps with a whip, and the left holding the reins. The horse is galloping. The lines of the wheel and a quiver, an imitation of a real war chariot, are carelessly incised. Traces of pink paint remain on the monkey.

On the reverse, in the mirror, the monkey faces right. Its head and shoulder have been rubbed away, but pink remains on the body and one visible arm, held up as on the other side. The quiver and wheel are incised, but the design is rough and confused. A hole is drilled through the piece near the bottom of the wheel, and if the front of the block had another in that position, two transverse sticks with wheels on them could have made the "chariot" mobile.

16. Monkey statuettes; one monkey drives a chariot, others are at play. The reverse view is shown in the mirror. (H. 8 cm.).

Statuette of Eight Monkeys

Unusually designed with two layers, this statuette shows four small monkeys above four larger ones. Two monkeys are seated side by side each end of the base with their outer arms stretched to meet around a large shape that is dented by their encirclement of it. The shape also bulges above their knees from the pressure of their legs braced against it, and suggests a bag of produce, nuts (?). The four smaller monkeys on the top layer are also two a

[UC 017]
Provenance: Amarna. Painted limestone. Height 9·0 cm. Width 5·6 cm. Depth 2·0 cm. Unpublished.

side, three seated and one standing on top of the sack. Their legs also make an impression on it in places, but their arms, although outstretched on one side, are not around it. They could be playing with each other, or about to forage for the produce squeezed up by the elders below. There is a hole through the piece between the smaller monkeys, possibly to clarify the design which is lively and unusual. The limestone has a brown coating with faint traces of red paint on some of the figures.

THREE MONKEY STATUETTES

17. *Three monkey statuettes with young animals, one with a pile of dates(?). The reverse is shown in the mirror. (H. 5·5 to 6·5 cm.).*

Two monkeys in left group

In the pyramidal group on the left, a large monkey, facing right, embraces a baby monkey which faces her while straddling a trussed bird. The piece is rounded and carved on the front and back but not identically. The base is an oval.

The left angle of the design is formed by the sloping back of the larger animal, and part of its head is now broken, as it bends over the smaller animal in its arms. The smaller monkey whose head is missing is crouching with bent arms and legs on the bird, and bending forward, making the sloping angle of the right side. A hole is pierced through the base. With realistic naturalism, the carving expresses a protective, perhaps family affection.

Centre group

In the centre of the plate is a rounded group of a larger monkey facing left, and a smaller one which, on the obverse, clings to an unidentifiable bottle-shaped object. This has a tall oval body in the round, with a rounded

[UC 032]
Provenance: Amarna. Limestone. Height 6·0 cm. Width 6·0 cm. Depth 2·0 cm. Unpublished.

39

[UC 033]
Provenance: Amarna. Painted lime-
stone. Height 6·5 cm. Width 4·0 cm.
Depth 2·5 cm. Comparison:
[1]M.D.O.G., No. 52, pl. 2. Cairo,
Ent. No. 44.866.

[UC 026]
Provenance: Amarna. Painted lime-
stone. Height 5·5 cm. Width 5·0 cm.
Depth 1·5 cm. Unpublished.

top. The oval base is now broken across the front; red paint remains on the figures, particularly on the unidentified shape.

The larger monkey is seated, elbows on knees, with its hands either side of the top of the tall shape, to which its mouth is attached. It might be supposed to be gnawing the stopper off a wine or beer jar, but the smaller monkey clings to the side of this as though it were soft. This, and the overall look of the piece suggests that the larger animal might be kissing the face of an unmodelled figure and that it could be a parody of the many scenes of the King kissing one of his daughters.[1] It bears a striking resemblance to an unfinished statue on this subject. In another monkey statuette in the Collection (UC 020), the snout of the larger animal is unmistakably joined to that of a smaller monkey on its knee.

Monkey with a Pile of Produce

Right of the plate, the monkey, facing left, is seated on an oval base along which its tail lies on the obverse side. Its legs are bent, feet braced against, and right arm round, a pile of dates (?) reaching to its chin. The left forearm is raised, either to steady the pile of fruit or take some to its mouth; in a similar statuette (UC 025) the monkey carries the fruit to its mouth in both hands.

The animal's upright back forms the right edge of the piece, the pile of fruit making the sloping left side. The body is well realised, the eyes carefully carved and the mouth and whiskers incised. The head has been replaced.

Traces of red paint remain on the statuette and the fruit, but this is one of these statuettes which shows signs of having been burnt, possibly after being discarded on one of the waste heaps which were apparently levelled at Amarna, and burnt off from time to time.

Reliefs

EARLY STYLE OF AMARNA RELIEF OF NEFERTITI

Although the mannerisms of the early Amarna style coarsen and age Nefertiti's features in this sunk relief, which was evidently carved when she was comparatively young, the rounded forms of her figure convey a flesh-like softness.

18. Early Amarna relief of Nefertiti wearing a Theban wig and disk with horns. (H. 13 cm.).

[UC 038]
Provenance: Amarna. Marble. Height
13·0 cm. Width 4·5 cm. Lit. J. Samson,
C/A III, p. 224, pl. CV (10).

The Queen faces left on a splinter of marble probably from a temple scene. In the conventional way, her shoulders are shown frontally, and her right breast in profile, but her left breast seems to have been unusually emphasised in a frontal position. A guide-line remains drawn from the left shoulder diagonally across the body. Her left arm is lost and the right one held out, possibly making an offering to the Aten. The uraeus is cursorily incised on a Theban type of wig, surmounted by the disk and horns of Isis. The ear is large and prominent as in the early Amarna reliefs. The bones of the face are modelled and an ageing line drawn from nostril to mouth, another early innovation. The eyebrow is deeply cut but the eye is subtly suggested by "bruising" the stone, perhaps unfinished, but certainly in a shape which is animated by light and shadow. The heavily carved profile has an outer line round the lips and makes strong shadows which give depth and form to the relief.

This is an example which reveals the change that took place in the Amarna age, from the previous artistic conception of carving religious scenes for the darkness of traditional temples, to the new demand for scenes dedicated to the sun in the direct light of unroofed buildings. The background shapes, the handling of the features, the heavily cut and angled outlines of the body, in contrast to the lighter stress laid on the crown and the even fainter lines of the wig, give a deliberate emphasis in a bright light. The carving is probably contemporary with the Queen's portrait on the balustrade from the Palace, but the handling of Amarna carving in religious scenes appears to be related to their individual significance and the effect of light and shadow.

Plate 20

(particularly visible on Plates 24 and 25)

NEFERTITI IN HER TALL CROWN

[UC 011]
Provenance: Amarna. Limestone, with
ink drawing, and carving. Height 8·5
cm. Width 7·0 cm. Lit. P. T/A., p. 30,
par. 72. J. Samson, C/A III, p. 225,
pl. CV (3).

In this bold ink drawing of Nefertiti in her prime the Queen wears the tall crown as in the best known Berlin portrait. Her profile, facing right, is on an unevenly squared piece of limestone with bevelled edges which may have been prepared for the master sketch. The edge behind the Queen is broken.

The portrait is outlined with masterly fluency. Lines running down the crown and around its edges and the uraeus are faultlessly placed. The almond shaped outline of the eye has the cosmetic line added and the line of a fold in the eye-lid touched in. One continuous brush stroke sweeps across the cap band on the brow and down the profile. Guide lines mark the lower plane of the jaw, two neck wrinkles, and the back of the neck which gives the recognisable forward poise of the Queen's head, all apparently for a sculptor to follow.

Carving has been started on the nostril, lips and chin, but false lines by the ear, perhaps carved by a pupil, are not properly placed for it or for an ear-ring and may have caused the work to be abandoned.

The drawing has the naturalism of the portrait heads in the round from Thutmose's studio, and it reveals the artistic certainty underlying such masterpieces.

42

19. *Nefertiti in her tall crown typical of many of her portraits from Amarna.* (*H. 8·5 cm.*).

ROYAL FIGURE ON A PALACE BALUSTRADE

This heavy alabaster section is from one of the balustrades that bordered the ramps in the central palace. It is a sunk relief, *en creux*, with the familiar scene of Akhenaten and Nefertiti offering to the Aten, followed by Meritaten, playing her sistrum. All face right and stand under the beneficent rays of the Aten. The relief, although broken above the King's shoulders, clearly shows the deeply cut ribs on the streamer which hangs down from his head-dress. On the King's upper arms, chest and waist, double cartouches are incised, showing the early form of the Aten names. The Queen wears an informal "bag" wig. Between her two uplifted hands, she offers an unguent vase which is blessed by a hand of the Aten; another touches her head, while, between them, a third brings the ʿ*ankh* to the uraeus on her brow. Seven other rays ending in hands descend to the three unguent vases on the offering table in front of the King. The two nearest the centre hang almost straight as though from the sun's disk (above the break). The depth of the cutting, and the angling of the carving is varied to achieve the full effect of light and shadow on the scene.

[UC 401]

Provenance: Central Palace at Amarna; early years Egyptian alabaster. Height 56·0 cm. Width 52·0 cm. Lit. W. M. F. Petrie, *T/A*, p. 8, pl. XII (3); p. 11 (19), pl. XII (4). J. D. S. Pendlebury, *C/A III* p. 66 and p. 77, pl. LXIX (4 and 5). Comparisons: [1]Cairo, E. Drioton, *Encyclopédie Photographique de l'Art*, p. 40.

Before the Queen's skirt is inscribed:—

Nfr-nfrw-itn Nfrt-itỉ ʿ*nḫ ḏt nḥḥ.*

"Nefer-neferu-aten Nefertiti, living forever and ever."

Above her head are the ends of two columns of large hieroglyphs, ending:

1. ....*n t3wy*   2. ....*ḏt nḥḥ*

" ....(Mistress?) of the Two Lands"   .... "for ever and ever".

Over the princesses, a vertical column reads:

.....*Mrt-(itn) ms.n ḥmt-nswt wrt Nfr-nfrw-itn Nfrt-itỉ* ʿ*nḫ.tỉ ḏt nḥḥ*

". . . . Merit(aten), born of the Great Royal Wife, Nefer-neferu-aten, Nefertiti, living forever and ever."

This section of the balustrade, originally in fragments, has been somewhat clumsily restored with plaster.

The block was found standing with another in the eastern doorway between the Broad Hall and the first State Apartment. The style of the art, with the disproportionately large hips, narrow waist and thin legs of the King and Queen and the distortion of her features, is little different from the Boundary Stelae. This, with the very childlike figure of Meritaten and the probable position of the balustrade in the palace, suggest it was carved early in the preparation of the city. Other sections of balustrades in limestone, purple sandstone, and black and red granite decorated the ramps leading up to the unusual architectural feature of raised doorways, and this suggests they were emphasised as focal points. They would have enabled Akhenaten and Nefertiti to pause in their long procession through the palace and "appear" above the heads of assembled audiences, as they entered and left the succession of State Apartments leading to the throne, a more intimate version of their royal appearances to the public outside the palace.

This block is roughly squared at the bottom, and at both sides, to fit beside other sections of the balustrade. On this one, the family stands on a gently rising line; in a similar Cairo block, the base-line is a descending one, parallel to the top.[1] As on the Deir-el-Bahri ramps, the supporting walls evidently took the change in gradient, leaving the balustrades at a fixed height. Comparisons show they reached a height of 1·18 metres.

20. The King, Queen and princess probably Meritaten, shown on an alabaster balustrade from the Central Palace, offering to the Aten. (H. 56 cm.).

FIGURE OF NEFERTITI FROM MEMPHIS

This early portrait of Nefertiti in coloured sunk relief was found by Petrie on the site of the Temple of Ptah in Memphis. Its style and dress distinguish it from early portraits of the Queen in the same pose from Thebes and Amarna, and it appears to be a rare example of an Amarna royal portrait from the north.

The limestone block is squared on the right side, at the base and on the top which is chipped, but the left side has been completely broken away. The Queen, facing left, stands at the end of what was almost certainly an Aten scene, with a slim column behind her. The damage on the left has removed the front of her face, broken the right shoulder, and taken the right arm, lower left arm and the left of her semi-profile body, which the end of the block cuts at hip level. She wears the long Theban type of wig with a fillet which was probably surmounted by a diadem. The hair is carved in detail; one lappet falls over her left breast and the rest behind her left shoulder. The ear is large and, typical of the early period, is shown prominently on top of the wig. There are traces of the uraeus on the brow and shapes which, by comparison with other reliefs (especially one in the Cleveland Museum), suggest that there was an Aten hand in front of it and possibly another carrying the ʿankh to her nose.[1]

21. This figure of Nefertiti is rare because Petrie found it at Memphis and she wears a skirt which differs from her portraits from Thebes and Amarna. (H. 20 cm.).

The top of the brow, the almond eye, and simply carved eyebrow, although chipped, are clearly visible. The front of the face is missing, but if it was originally carried forward on the same plane as the remaining cheek, it would seem to have been shown as smooth and more fitting to a young woman than to the gaunt and lined portraits of the young Queen from the southern capitals. The frontal shoulders and three-quarters right breast are

45

rounded; the upper left arm, bent across the body to the waist, was probably raised with an offering to the Aten in the Queen's hands, as in so many examples.[2] On the arm is a pair of cartouche-plaques with the early form of the Aten name used before year 9; a similar pair on the right breast are partly broken away by the damage to the shoulder.

The dress is not typical of a Theban or of an Amarna Queen's robe. There is no suggestion of a necklace, and the pleated sash around her waist with a cross-ribbed tie falling from the centre is reminiscent of the style of sash worn by Menkheper, Mayor of Memphis, in the previous reign.[3] It presumably held up her skirt.

The smashing of the left side of the block may have obliterated the figure of the King who usually precedes her, and certainly all signs of the Aten. The gash behind her head occurs in the position where an Aten hand often appears, and was probably to obliterate the symbol.

Pale red paint remains on her face and body and the portrait gives an impression of relaxed elegance rather than the more rigid crudity of early reliefs of the Queen from Thebes and Amarna.

[UC 037]
Provenance: Temple of Ptah, Memphis. Amarna Period. Painted limestone. Height 20·0 cm. Width 18·5 cm. Lit. W. M. F. Petrie, *Riqqeh and Memphis, VI*, p. 32, pl. LIV (9), 1915. Comparisons: [1]*Cleveland Museum Bulletin*, No. 59, 186, fig. 6, Jan. 1968; [2]J. D. S. Pendlebury, *C/A III*, pl. LXVI (1); [3]W. C. Hayes, *Scepter of Egypt, II*, p. 272, fig. 166, MMA., N.Y., 1968.

SITAMEN FROM THEBES

[UC 14373]
Provenance: Temple of Amenophis II/III, Thebes, Dynasty XVIII, c. 1380 B.C. Painted sandstone. Height 51·0 cm. Width 49·0 cm. Lit. W. M. F. Petrie, *Six Temples at Thebes*, pp. 6 and 11, pl. VI (8), 1897.

22. Sitamen from Thebes. (H. 51 cm.)

On this large sandstone block, the *bas-relief* carving of a Queen is unfinished. Above her head, in the lower left corner of a broken cartouche, are the back and legs of the *s3* bird and part of a *t* from the name Sitamen. Beside it is the bottom of a column of inscription with only the *t* remaining legible. Above this and at an angle down the right side, the block is broken. The left side and lower edge are squared.

Sitamen faces right. She wears the vulture head-dress with the head and body of the bird carved in detail, but the lappet, which falls from the head-dress down on to her breast, and the three-cornered "streamer", which flares out from it at the back, are only blocked in, with traces of blue paint still remaining on them. The Queen wears a necklace of which only the edges are carved, the rows being shown by blue painted loops. Over her shoulders are the straps of her Theban gown from which her left breast protrudes by her left arm near the break in the stone, beyond which was presumably her sheath-like dress. Her face is carved without planes; the profile is clearly cut, the nostril modelled, and there is a trace of a smile on the full lips. The chin is firm and the carriage of the head regal. The eye is merely a recessed oval, with the cosmetic line from the outer edge, and the eyebrow raised in *bas-relief*. The Queen carries the royal "flail" with the lily terminal, which falls along the top line of her left arm.

Except for this queenly pose, the details of the portrait closely resemble the more finished, painted limestone relief of Hatshepsut's mother, 'Aḥmose, at Deir-el-Bahri, but both her arms drop straight down from her shoulders. The shallow *bas-relief* carving of Sitamen's portrait is in the tradition of XVIIIth Dynasty temple reliefs, and the vulture head-dress of a royal heiress, God's Wife of Amen, is the same as that worn by pre-Amarna Queens of this Dynasty. The relief was found by Petrie in the Theban temple of Amenophis II, which was later remodelled by Amenophis III; this relief has been associated with his daughter, Sitamen. Described as both his daughter and his wife, her rôle in her father's entourage was evidently that of royal heiress. Possibly an official marriage was arranged between them, perhaps to secure a male heir, as Àkhenaten and Nefertiti apparently had only daughters, and Queen Ty, although so powerful, was born a commoner.

The carving may have been taken over by Amenophis III, by adding a relevant inscription. So reminiscent of queens who occur earlier in the Dynasty, it provides a contrast to royal portraiture later in his reign and in the Amarna period. Sitamen, the royal heiress, is monumentally majestic, impersonal, and ageless.

PROFILE OF AKHENATEN

On a limestone slab, squared both sides and at the bottom but broken diagonally across the top, is the lower half of the profile of a King in shallow sunk relief. The break on the left is above the ear and, on the right, above the nostril. The King faces right, and strongly resembles portraits of Akhenaten.

The carving is in the best tradition of Amarna reliefs. The nostril is sensitive, the lips full but not coarse, and the chin is bony without the exaggeration of the early period. The face is delicately modelled but the

Plate 23

[UC 402]
Provenance: By the sculptor's place near the southern end of the town, Amarna. Limestone. Height 17·0 cm. Width 19·0 cm. Lit. P. *T/A*, p. 31, pl. 1 (5) and p. 11. Comparison: G. Roeder, *Amarna Reliefs aus Hermopolis*, pl. 5. 255-VI, Hildesheim, 1969.

47

subtle gradation of the planes is masked by the pitted surface of the stone. Two folds are shown on the front of the neck in Amarna tradition, but the front line of the neck is not continued down to the break in the stone. On the left, the ear is less well carved than the rest of the face, with an unduly deep rounded cavity, similar to those which were shown pierced through the lobe, needed for the shanks of Amarna ear-rings. On this ear, however, the lobe is not fully carved. Behind the ear is the base of the Blue Crown and the turn at the back of the thin neck.

23. Profile of Akhenaten in the Amarna style without the exaggeration of the early Karnak portraits. (H. 17 cm.).

Petrie records the finding of the piece by the sculptor's place near the south end of the town (Thutmose's(?)), and describes it as "the head of Akhenaten on a slab which does not appear to have come from any building and is probably a trial (piece)." The unfinished line at the base of the neck gives it this appearance and, found so near the studio, it may have been a "copy book" sample. It is comparable with a relief of Akhenaten from Hermopolis. Although this is on a larger block with more of the King's body showing, and it has more stylised carving, there are sufficient parallels for both pieces to have been based on the same or similar model of the King's profile.

24. This offering by a Queen of a libation to the Aten is enhanced by the variation of carving techniques which emphasise her gesture. (H. 15·2 cm.).

A QUEEN OFFERS LIBATION TO THE ATEN

On an unevenly broken block of purple quartzite, a Queen, probably Nefertiti, is following a King whose shoulder and the streamers from his crown are in front of her. The stone is finely prepared and polished and the carving is notable for a combination of techniques giving emphasis from strong light and shadow.

The Queen faces left and in her upraised hands offers to the Aten a typical libation vessel with a short spout. Two rays from the Sun-God descend

49

[UC 040]
Provenance: Amarna, Great Temple
(?). Purple quartzite. Height 15·2 cm.
Width 10·0 cm. Lit. J. Samson, C/A
III, p. 225, pl. CV (6). Comparison:
J. D. S. Pendlebury, C/A III, p. 11,
Great Temple.

diagonally across the surface, the upper one with a hand on the end blessing the uraeus on the Queen's brow; the lower ray passes behind the Queen's head, giving a three-dimensional effect. The broken right edge of the block cuts across the wig and face of the Queen in front of the ear. The head is carved in sunk relief.

The front of the "Nubian" wig and the uraeus catch the light. The top outline of the profile, eyebrow and eye are deeply carved to give deep shadow in a top, left light, but this illumines the brow and eyelid and the lines under the nostril and chin and between the lips. The planes of the face are natural without the sunken and lined appearance of the exaggerated "Amarna" style, and allows only a slight shadow under the cheek-bone. The Aten rays are deeply cut, and the straight sides catch light on one edge. Further emphasis is given to the religious meaning of the relief by combining different carving techniques around the offering. The Queen's uplifted forearms are rounded between the sunken edges, but her left hand, which supports the libation vessel, is in raised relief against the recessed stone of the streamers from the King's crown. The right hand is in sunk relief, but raised along the fore-finger, and these variations would focus the eye on the offering in any light. Two Aten plaques on the Queen's right arm are uninscribed.

Pendlebury believed this may be a fragment from the great "purple" stela of which he found many pieces in the unroofed temple, where the combined carving techniques would show to advantage, and give emphasis to the religious ritual.

A LIBATION OFFERING TO THE ATEN

*Plate 24

In a painted relief on this roughly rectangular limestone fragment, which is broken on all four edges, significance is given to a libation which is being offered to the Aten, by employing various carving techniques, similar to the offering above.*

[UC 24281] (W)
Provenance: The Broad Hall, central
palace, Amarna. Painted limestone.
Height 15·0 cm. Width 14·0 cm.
J. D. S. Pendlebury's excavation
reference, C/A III, (265), p. 68.

25. Both the carving of this relief and the painting of the sun's rays red against the white limestone intensify this libation offering to the Aten. (H. 15 cm.).

50

The neck of the libation vase is broken at the top left of the block, but the body of the vase is held upright on an elongated hand with long fingers and back-turned top joints, typical of royal hands in so many reliefs at Amarna. Three rays from the Aten descend diagonally towards the left, with narrowing distances between them as they near the centre (under the sun's disk). The ray on the left passes behind the vessel and the hand, and gives a three-dimensional effect that is heightened by the rounded shape of the vase which is recessed at the sides. Between recessed outlines, the sun's rays are rounded, and traces remain on them of the red paint; this stresses the pattern they make against the very white smooth limestone. Colour is used here to give the emphasis achieved by the deep squared cutting of the rays on the offering Plate 24 above. The hand and fingers are in sunk relief, with red paint remaining around them, but by recessing the bottom of the vessel, the thumb is shown in *bas-relief*, so as to catch the light from all angles.

The relief was found in the unroofed Broad Hall of the central palace, and increases the evidence of the skill which went into the royal and religious scenes at Amarna.

AN EARLY AMARNA PORTRAIT OF A PRINCESS

[UC 083]
Provenance: Amarna. Diorite. Height 15·0 cm. Width 10·0 cm. Unpublished.

26. *Although she is only small and young the angularity of this early Amarna portrait of a princess, ages her. (H. 15 cm.) Unpublished.*

This angular carving of a princess, on a heavy, unevenly broken block of diorite with only part of the right edge unbroken, has all the signs of one of the earliest carvings in the building of Amarna. It probably shows Meritaten, the eldest princess; she is at the end of a scene, closely following her mother, whose gown, apparently below the hips, can be seen in front of the princess next to and above her head. The carving of what was presumably Nefertiti's figure appears to be on a big scale; the princess's figure is relatively small, suggesting that she was a young child. Her exaggerated and projecting adult features and her attenuated body with its almost wizened appearance, so like the disproportion of the portraits from the early Aten days at Thebes, endorses the early date.

Although so young, she is elaborately dressed, perhaps attending an official Aten ceremony. She holds the princess' sistrum in her right hand just above her head; the left arm is hanging in a typical manner by her side. Both arms are match-stick thin and her waist is little broader. She wears the side-lock of youth, a collar-necklace and a gown draped across her chest with pleats down the skirt. The block is broken at her knees. Above her head an ḥ sign remains, from the prayer for eternal life at the end of a column of inscription. The angularity of this figure can be compared with the more flowing lines of the princess in the scene on a column from the central palace, for which there is evidence of a later date.

Plate 27

A PRINCESS FROM A CENTRAL PALACE COLUMN

In Akhenaten's central palace, described by Pendlebury as the largest secular building in the ancient world and the only one built of stone, he found this fragment in the first inner court, south of the Broad Hall.[1] The highly polished, light honey coloured quartzite is part of a band that encircled a column some two feet in diameter.

The princess is carved in low relief and faces left. She was evidently part of a scene of the royal family as described by Petrie on the bands encircling the columns in the harem court.[2] Her right arm is raised, presumably to hold a sistrum above her head; her left hangs down by her side. She wears the side-lock of youth over an apparently shaven head or possibly on a cap (with the side-lock attached to it). A large collar-necklace hangs over her gown which is draped across her left breast with the pleats gathered at the waist and hanging down over the hips, leaving the front of the figure bare. The sloping break in the stone is under the buttock and above the knees.

Despite the heavy face, and the disproportion of the attenuated stock pose of the figure, the style of the carving suggests it was a later work than that of the princess on page 51; the less angular lines of the figure offer a greater contrast than can be explained by the softer stone alone, and there are pointers to it being carved at a later period at Amarna, when the royal daughters were growing up. The princess on the fragment is possibly Meritaten, as she appears to be immediately following her mother, whose robe can be seen on the left lower corner of the fragment, and she is taller in relation to this indication of her mother's figure than she was on page 51. Behind her is apparently the elbow of another princess with arm upheld, presumably with a sistrum, who is also relatively tall. Furthermore, the fragment was found

[UC 24279] (W)
Provenance: First State Apartment of the Central Palace, Amarna. Yellow quartzite. Height 17·0 cm. Width 14·0 cm. Lit. [1]J. D. S. Pendlebury's excavation note, C/A III, (No. 100), p. 68. Comparison: [2]P. T/A, p. 10, pl. 1. Unpublished.

Plate 26

Plate 26

in the Court where Pendlebury uncovered the foundations of a temporary brick structure which he identified as the office of the architect who was directing the building of the State Apartments. He believed that these could not have been finished before year 9 and as this Court would have had to wait completion until after the brick shelter was removed, it was possibly one of the last sections to be finished. If the fragment belonged to the court in which it was found, it would endorse the assessment of a middle date for the piece on grounds of style and the relative sizes of the princesses.

27. From a scene on a Central Palace column. This princess is holding up a sistrum. The flowing lines of the figure suggest it is later than plate 26. (H. 17 cm.).

TWO OFFERING BEARERS

Two offering bearers in this painted, sunk relief face right, as they carry fruit and flowers to an altar or at a temple ceremony. The block is dressed stone at the top and on the right but unevenly broken at the bottom and left side. The scene shows a number of the innovations that characterise Amarna art.

28. *Two offering bearers with fruit and flowers.* (H. 33 cm.).

The bearers are carved with the shaven heads of temple attendants and wear the usual pleated skirt and central tie, but, typical of the best Amarna scenes, although they were presumably subordinate figures in a scene among many officials, they are carved as individuals. Both men are shown with their slightly differing heads and faces in profile and their skulls recessed around the ear, which emphasises their bare heads. Their frontal shoulders and nearly profile bodies retain the conventions of traditional Egyptian art. But although this subject in previous reigns is mostly shown by repetitive figures carrying different offerings, here, the man on the left bends forward more than the

54

other bearer and although they carry virtually the same produce, the design is varied and carved to suggest movement and depth.

The bearer on the left holds in his right hand a large XVIIIth Dynasty bouquet sheath made with layers of stalks bound together. This rests on his right shoulder and fits behind his head, accentuating the projecting back of his skull, giving a three-dimensional effect. From the top of the sheath a large papyrus flower emerges, notched around the rim and recessed at both sides giving another illusion of depth. This, though partly broken away, is flanked right and left by two buds. The man's left arm is held out before him with a basket or tray of offerings balanced on his nearly horizontal forearm. On this tray are two layers of figs on top of three pomegranates, all upright in profile. This pile of fruit almost covers the body of the second bearer who is shorter, which gives a degree of perspective to the design. From the top of his right shoulder and presumably held in his right hand are three rectangular stylised bouquet "cones" with slightly curved tops designed as though fitting into one another; these are also recessed both sides. The use of such floral cones is apparently demonstrated on the raised border of the stela, where lotuses and buds emerge from the shapes, and loops. From the cones rises a larger papyrus head than on the left, notched at the rim, recessed at both sides and flanked by two buds.

The tray carried by this bearer and some of the produce on it was apparently continued over the edge of the block into the next one, suggesting well fitted masonry minimising the crack between. On the tray are horizontal layers of bread (?), under three layers of upright figs, topped by a large bouquet of papyrus flowers with the stalks twisted and bound into a loop and then hanging down each side of the fruit. From the trays hang branches of leaves. There are traces of red paint on these and occasional touches remaining on the figures.

Across the top of the limestone is a line possibly dividing this from a register above. If these bearers are part of an Aten ritual with the royal family shown in the relatively large proportion in which they appear in the Amarna tombs, the scale of the relief suggests a very large and extensive scene.[1] If they formed part of the preparation of an altar for royal worship, the scale indicates its importance, perhaps in a temple.

The movement in this composition in which the bearers appear to be pressing forward highlights the difference between them and offering bearers in Theban tombs like Ramose's in the previous reign where they are shown in a repetitive line of stereotyped faces and figures like a design in a beautiful frieze.[2] In this scene the forward impetus is suggested by the pose of the figures and intensified by the angles of the shapes between them which mostly point forward. This action in the composition, the individualism of the figures, and the illusion of depth inherent in the placing of objects, the recession of their sides and the diminishing size of the man further from the front, show some of the innovations in the art of the Amarna period.

[UC 405]
Provenance: Amarna. Painted limestone. Height 33·0 cm. Width 33·0 cm. Depth 7·5 cm. Unpublished. Comparisons: [1]N. de G. Davies, *RTA*, *II*, pl. XVIII, London, 1905; [2]N. de G. Davies, *Tomb of Vizier Ramose*, pl. XLIV and XLVI, London, 1941.

Plate 55a

FIGURE FROM THE TOMB OF AY

The unfinished figure of a servant facing left on this roughly squared block of limestone has the remains of yellow paint on it which evidently once

55

covered the figure. The face in profile is simply carved; the nose is shaped but the eye and mouth little more than incised, although the expression is one of animation undestroyed by the flaked and chipped stone. The head is lifted slightly, the right arm, carved to the elbow, is raised in evident acclaim and the left, carved to the wrist, swings out behind the figure. A "Nubian" wig is shaped with a long back-line; the figure wears the pubic sheath with a narrow tie round the waist as worn by soldiers, sentries, charioteers and grooms. The shoulders are shown frontally and the abdomen and legs in three-quarter view, but the pose is active, looking or perhaps even moving to the left.

29. *An unfinished but welcoming figure from the tomb of Ay. (H. 29 cm.).*

Petrie described the block as one of a curious class he found in the city, carved on slabs of limestone rudely smoothed at the sides but rounded at the corners which would preclude a good join.[1] He did not know that the tomb robbers had squared the reliefs they hacked from the tomb walls and apparently dropped some of the blocks in the plain. This figure has been traced to a scene on the north wall of Ay's tomb. It was removed between 1843-45, when it was included *in situ* in the drawings for the *Denkmäler* of Lepsius, and 1891-2, when Petrie found it in the city.

The figure is one of a group welcoming Ay as he returns from court laden with honours bestowed by the King and Queen in the previous scene. The three figures nearest Ay were damaged, but this one, perhaps a groom in the service of Ay, the King's Master of Horse, was completely hacked out. The workmanship is rough, the figure unimportant, but it has the involvement typical in crowd scenes at Amarna, and expresses the movement of a genuine participant in a moment of rejoicing.

[UC 409]
Provenance: Amarna. Painted limestone. Height 29·0 cm. Width 24·0 cm. Lit. [1]P. *T/A.*, 11, pl. XI.

A FOOD CARRIER

Although the shaven hair of this man carrying provisions on his head suggests he may be bringing them to an Aten altar in a temple, it is also possible he was carrying food in a palace scene. The figure faces left in a coloured sunk relief on a jagged block of limestone probably hacked from a wall; the surface is badly damaged. The block is broken in front of and behind the figure, above the provisions, and below the face.

30. In this relief the pile of food on the bearer's head is carved into the register above him, an Amarna variation. (H. 9·5 cm., W. 15 cm.).

The modelled features are Egyptian. The slightly turned up nose and thick nostril in the profile which is carved with an open mouth, has a coarseness accentuated by a lump of stone left between the lips. The oval eye is recessed, enabling a deep shadow from the brow, and a highlight on the lid. The skull is recessed around the ear which is roughly carved. At the back of the head is the beginning of the neck; in front, the profile ends at the chin. The provisions of two loaves under a fish (?) are set, perhaps carelessly or for purposes of design, on the back half of the man's head. They appear to extend into the register above the figure, suggested by two horizontal lines across the block in front of the bottom loaves, behind which the surface of the stone is missing. This varying of a composition by extending the forms across the rigid register-lines is one of the innovations at Amarna which gives the reliefs their liveliness. In the top left corner above the lines is unidentifiable carving, with red and yellow paint. Red and yellow paint remain on the provisions and red on the head.

[UC 017]

Provenance: Amarna. Painted limestone. Height 9·5 cm. Width 15·0 cm. Lit. J. Samson, C/A III, p. 227, pl. CVI (3).

The block has not been squared like those plundered from the tombs and its condition suggests it may have been shattered when quarried from a wall in the city. Little of the surface stone remains around the carving except behind the head, where it is angled in a forward point. The relief is more crudely presented than the offering bearers, but the incisive design expresses action.

FOREIGNERS ON A LIMESTONE BALUSTRADE

Decorated on both sides with a frieze of foreigners, probably captives, this carved block of limestone with the smoothed top is apparently the end block of a balustrade, possibly from one of the many ramps or stairways of the central palace. It has one end bevelled and the other roughly flattened. The rounded or "roll" top with the ridge at the sides is typical of the larger balustrades with decorated sides, found in varying stone, as discussed on page 44. On this less important limestone example, the stone at the top of the finished end slopes outwards to meet a smoothed vertical, while the other end is roughly squared, presumably to fit against the next segment. The work is roughly executed.

[UC 069]

Provenance: Amarna. Painted limestone relief. Bevelled end to unfinished surface 11·0 cm. Front surface width 12·5 cm. Height 7·0 cm. Diameter across roll top to side ridges 12·0 cm.

The parallel sides are decorated with the painted heads of foreigners in coarse, sunk relief. They face away from the bevelled end, presumably in a procession along the balustrade, and as the height of the block is only some 7 centimetres, it can be assumed that the rest of their figures was carved on the upright sides now broken away.

Plate 31

On the obverse, is the top of the head of a Libyan, broken from below his ear. In front of the ear is the side-lock, and rising from the top of his head, are the two feathers of his head-dress with the streamer falling down the back. Only the brow of his face remains. There are traces of red paint on the head. Behind him is the front half of a negro's head, with part of the hair, the brow, nose and upper lip, but the cheek has broken away. The centre of the head reaches the finished edge of the section. Red paint remains in squares incised on his head, suggesting crinkly hair or a wig. On the reverse is the

Plate 32

whole of a profile head of a negro, with the same squared head-dress and remains of red paint on it. The lips are thick, nose spreading and brow receding and he wears the large round ear-ring hanging from his ear. The block is broken at the base of his neck. Behind him is an indistinguishable curved shape, possibly of a partial figure like the one ending the procession on the obverse.

The working of the stone of this block is unusually poor, possibly showing haste in finishing parts of the buildings which were not the State Apartments or important sections, but the national characteristics of the foreigners are appreciated and faithfully represented.

PROFILE OF A MAN

33. The carving of a master. On the reverse there are trial carvings of students. (H. 20 cm.).

[UC 013]
Provenance: A sculptor's place near the south end of the town, Amarna. Limestone. Height 20·0 cm. Width 14·5 cm. Lit. P. *T/A.*, p. 30, pl. 1 (6); *History of Egypt, II.* p. 182, fig. 115, London, 1899. J. Samson, *C/A III*, p. 225, pl. CV (2).

Petrie found this profile relief, which is on a fine piece of limestone, at a sculptor's workshop near the south end of the town, possibly Thutmose's. The head faces left and retains an arresting distinction despite a joined break, across the stone at eye level, and other fractures.

The wig is a typical Amarna shape with the point in this case by the front of the neck. The features are not without resemblance to the royal family but no insignia is shown and it is unlikely to be Queen Ty to whom it was once assigned. The nose is carved with care, the lips droop slightly and a downward line is drawn from the outer corner; the chin and jaw line are well defined. The eye is carved with the particular detail found in good Amarna reliefs. The eyebrow is recessed and the eyelid shown by an outward turn over the almond-shaped eye. The planes of the face mark the cheek bone.

On the reverse are trials of features, a profile and hieroglyphs. Two separate eyes are carved, one in the form used in the profile and the other perhaps by a pupil. There is the ovoid head and profile of an Amarna princess; three pairs of full lips have been carved, one possibly by the master and two with less success. Of two *nb* signs, one shows the weave of the basket.

TWO PROFILES ON A TRIAL PIECE

Two profile reliefs of young men facing right have been carved on a block of limestone squared at the right and top and bottom, but broken on the left side. The lower profile is more expertly carved. The outline is faultless; the wig is firmly placed by a line at the top across the brow and another down the face and neck; a line under the recessed eyebrow divides it from the eyelid over the almond-shaped eye. The nose and full lips are modelled and the planes of the face skilfully shown in a young and fairly full cheek.

On the profile above, the same shaped wig is fully but unevenly outlined. Although the features are carved on the same model as below, which might be the master's copy, they lack the fineness. The surface of the stone of this head is more spotted than below, which to some extent masks the planes of the face, but these apparently have not been fully understood by the artist; for instance, the curved line above the lip lacks meaning.

[UC 037]
Provenance: Amarna. Limestone. Height 23·0 cm. Width 18·5 cm. Lit. J. Samson, *C/A III*, p. 225, pl. CV (1).

34. Two profiles on a trial piece. (H. 23 cm.).

SCULPTOR'S STUDIES OF HANDS

35. Sculptor's studies of hands. (H. 17 cm.).

The limestone block used as a trial piece for these studies of hands was badly broken at the top and left sides which have been mended with plaster. The right side and bottom of the block are squared. The studies are of three left hands, holding the roll or 'kerchief, which projects from under the little finger that is clenched, with the rest of the fingers in the palm of the hand.

The plaster covers a hand on the bottom left of the block except for the fleshy lower part of the palm, the wrist bone and lower arm which are life-like and make the example on its right look wooden. In this, the four fingers clasp the roll which is shown unfinished beyond the little finger; the thumb bends over the first finger but the palm reflects none of the pressure from the finger and the whole is carved without much indication of muscle or bone. The nails are shown in great detail with a double line encircling the quick.

Above this, the clenched hand in the same position has been given more shape in its palm and apparently had a wrist bone, but the stone here is broken. The top of the thumb is lost. The fingers are shown as pressing into the centre of the hand and the roll appears to be held by them but is in-expertly dealt with and where it emerges from under four fingers of nearly the same length gives the impression of a fifth finger. The nails are carved but not all with the detail of the hand below it.

Despite the apparently cursory treatment of some hands, even on major figures in Amarna reliefs, they were clearly studied in detail.

THE VARIED CARVING OF HIEROGLYPHS

The hieroglyphs carved on these two fragments of inscriptions on finely grained and highly polished quartzite, probably formed a part of the royal titulary. On the left the quail-chick, *w*, with part of the *šwt* plant, was possibly from *nsw* "King of Upper Egypt", while on the right is the pintail duck, perhaps part of *s3-rˁ* "the son of the sun" from Akhenaten's name.

The carving of the chick, which faces right, and the stem of the plant, is deep and straight sided, casting heavy shadows which would embolden a description to be seen from afar on an outside wall. The shoots each side of the stem are slender and graceful but catch the light on one edge. This bold treatment needs little detail within the outlines, and the base of the stem and the chick are only slightly modelled; the bird's beak is a thin incised line. Standing on a base-line the chick is given the perkiness of a small bird.

[UC 084 and 74]
Provenance: Amarna. Left fragment, pink quartzite. Height 11·5 cm. Width 9·5 cm. Right fragment, red quartzite. Height 12·0 cm. Width 7·5 cm. Unpublished.

In contrast, the pintail duck is flat footed and has the suggestion of a strut along its base-line. It faces right. The style of carving between two horizontal lines, with the remains of hieroglyphs in the lower register suggests that the inscription is part of one from the pedestal of a statue, or perhaps an indoor wall to be seen at close quarters. For this the outlines are shallower and the edges slightly turned back so that the light falls on the fuller and more detailed modelling of the bird's head, wing and breast, as well as the tail feathers which are partly lost by damage to the stone.

36. Examples of methods of carving hieroglyphs from two different sites. (H. 11·5 cm., W. 9·5 cm.; H. 12 cm., W. 7·5 cm.).

I. *Head of Nefertiti with preparation for tall crown to be added in another material.* (H. 6·5 cm.).

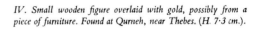

IV. *Small wooden figure overlaid with gold, possibly from a piece of furniture. Found at Qurneh, near Thebes.* (H. 7·3 cm.).

II. *Back of an ankle and heel in red jasper from a composite statue with robes in another stone as on the back of Tutankhamen's throne, plate 14b.* (H. 12 cm.).

III. *Composed of faience beads found separately at Amarna this necklace is assembled on the lines of those worn by both men and women. The beads include grapes, green leaves, green and blue cornflowers, red poppy petals, blue "drops," yellow mandrake fruits, red oval "dates" and white lotus petals, some tipped with blue.* (L. longest white petal 4·5 cm. Shortest cornflower 1·5 cm.).

V. *Figures of princesses—red moulded glass.* (H. 9 cm.).

INK SKETCH OF A STALKING BABOON

This apparently casual record in ink of a baboon prowling on all-fours has deft certainty and the economy of excellence that places it with the world's great sketches. Taking advantage of the smooth surface of a block of fine limestone, the artist has made a free sketch of the animal moving stealthily along to the right. One unbroken brush stroke runs from the tip of its tail along the back and down the right leg. The characteristics of its head and body are unmistakable and achieved with seven or eight strokes.

Many formal designs on walls, where drawings were prepared for the sculptor to carve, lack the immediacy of this quick sketch, but this lacks nothing of the observation and inspired line of the best work of the ancient Egyptian draughtsmen.

37. Ink sketch of a stalking baboon. (L. of drawing 4·2 cm.).

[UC 1585]
Provenance: Amarna. Ink sketch on limestone. The block, Height 7·5 cm. Width 16·0 cm. The length of baboon, Length 4·2 cm. Tail 5·0 cm. Lit. J. Samson, *C/A III*, p. 228.

Inlays

TWO ROYAL INLAYS WITH ROUND EDGED CARVING

Both these portraits are carved in the manner customary for stone inlays except that, on one the stone is worked around the front edge of the profile, with the same perfection as on the surface which suggests the turn of the face was meant to be seen. They would not have been easy to inlay flat into a wall like the head on p. 68, but could have been set with the front edge left above the surface.

Plate 38

38. Part of a royal inlay with carving round the edge. (H. 6 cm.).

In the broken fragment which faces right, the carving and colour continues for half a centimetre round the edge with the same finish as on the rest of the surface. The lips are coloured a soft red and rounded as though they were to lie against the surface rather than sink into it; the chin bulges at the back before it is flattened, which would keep the inlay raised. The shadow cast by the raised profile would have given it the depth which the relief carvers at

66

Amarna were seeking in their varied cutting. The surface of the stone has a warmer tone than the yellower colour at the back, probably from the effect of its extremely fine finish or perhaps from the faint remains of flesh colour-ing. No photograph fully shows the subtle modelling of the flesh over the chin or the soft planes of the jawline. The relaxed, sensuous, edged lips are slightly drooping at the corners with the fold of a half smile typical of some of the Amarna royal portraits. The contours of this face are softer and more feminine than those in the other head, and suggest it was part of an inlay portrait of Nefertiti.

39. A royal inlay head with edge carving prepared for the addition of a crown and features in other materials. (H. 9 cm.).

In the King's portrait, facing left, the surface abrasion partly masks the light modelling of the face which is faintly coloured with flesh-coloured paint, and the lips with light red. Although unfinished, the profile carving is carried round the front edge, suggesting the possibility of another raised inlay; it is shaped in much the same way as on a glass head for inlay. On the nose and lips, the dark paint guide-lines have not yet been cut away; these also remain in the eye and eyebrow recesses being prepared for separate inlays. The head is shaped for the addition of a separate crown; the lobe of the ear is pierced. The cheek is firm, but it is raised to reflect the beginning of the smile shown by a line at the corner of the mouth; the jaw-line is masculine compared with the other inlay.

Woolley found inlay portraits of the King and Queen in the chapel at Maruaten, one of which, now in the Ashmolean Museum, has rounded-edge carving similar to the King's profile.

Plate 45

[UC 102 and 101]
Provenance: Amarna. Yellow quartz-ite. Height of broken fragment 6·0 cm. Width 6·5 cm. (102). Height of King's inlay 9·0 cm. Width 9·0 cm. (101). Lit. J. Samson, C/A III, text, p. 226, pl. CV (4 and 7). Comparisons: C. L. Woolley, C/A I, p. 121, pl. XXXV (1 and 2), London, 1923; Ashmolean, No. 1922 (95).

40. A royal inlay with delicately carved face prepared for an inlaid eye and eyebrow and the addition of a crown. (H. 10 cm.).

[UC 103]
Provenance: Amarna. Yellow quartzite. Height 10·0 cm. Width 11·0 cm. Width across back 10·0 cm. Depth 6·0 cm. Lit. J. Samson, *C/A III*, text, p. 226, pl. CV. Comparisons: ¹Head of Smenkhkare, J. D. S. Pendlebury, *C/A III*, p. 12 (33/6), pl. LIX (6–8). Brooklyn inlay, 33.685.

Much of the quality of this inlay is lost in a photograph. The warm tan-coloured stone has been worked to a marble-smoothness and the planes of the face are so subtly carved that only by handling it can its full textural finish be appreciated. The profile faces left. It has a sharp edge and was evidently intended to be deeply set into a wall so that the face was flush with the surface. The ear is well carved and the lobe shown as pierced.

The eye socket and eyebrow are prepared for inlays and the head for a crown, with possibly a streamer inlaid in the triangular groove behind the ear. Such detail shows that the robes and regalia were added to some of the carefully wrought royal inlays at Amarna, making them composite figures like those inlaid on Tutankhamen's golden throne.

The lips which are painted red appear to have been lifted in a smile; they are not the full drooping feature familiar on many portraits of Akhenaten, Nefertiti, Ty and Tutankhamen. The features seem to have been shallower than Akhenaten's and the expression of resigned sweetness more characteristic of the statue head from the Great Temple, in the Brooklyn Museum and the inlay head in that Museum.¹

68

VI. Fragments of faience tiles and inlays of fruit, flowers and from figures. Mosaic fragments in the bottom row. (Tallest H. 7 cm.).

VII. Coloured faience tiles, a duck, fish and reeds from pool scenes. (Tallest H. 7·9 cm.).

VIII. Moulds, with relevant faience objects made in them or similar examples. (Triangular mould H. 6·6 cm.).

69

NON-ROYAL HEAD FOR INLAY

Coarse, very white limestone has been used for this head which faces right and is carved with a flat back for inlaying. The negroid characteristics of a prognathous jaw, thick lips, high cheek bones and a receding forehead are well observed and technical skill has been combined with artistic insight, in the carving. It is not a flat profile. The nose and lips are just turned around the edge giving a depth that is enhanced by the modelling of the eyebrow, the bridge of the nose and the shapely jaw line. These details, with the varied planes in the face, the wig and the typical ear-ring animate this head, which would have had significance even in a large wall scene.

To fit it well into the background, the tip of the nose and the end of the chin have been squared. As a non-royal portrait it is not carved to receive additional inlaid details in faience, stones or glass, as are the royal heads.

[UC 009]
Provenance: Amarna. Coarse limestone. Height 8·0 cm. Width 8·0 cm. Lit. J. Samson, *C/A III*, text, p. 227, pl. CVI (4).

41. Deeply carved non-royal head for inlay without preparation for additional features. (H. 8 cm.).

AN 'AMARNA' PRINCESS FROM THEBES

This small gilded wooden figure comes from Qurneh, near the Theban valley of the Tombs of the Kings, and in 1927, five years after Tutankhamen's tomb had been excavated there, Petrie wrote that it was "probably a daughter of Akhenaten".[1] Further study of it in comparison with details on some of Tutankhamen's furniture from his tomb strengthens this probability, and by its comparison with other figures, suggests that the youngest Amarna princesses went to live with Tutankhamen and his Queen, their older sister,

70

42. *The figure of Tutankhamen and Queen Ankhesenamen are carved and painted on this ivory lid and below them two royal ladies, probably the Queen's younger sisters, pick mandrakes in a garden.*

Facsimile of Plate IV. See p. 64.

after their parents died and the Court eventually returned to Thebes under Tutankhamen.

The small standing figure faces left. It is made of wood, coated with gesso and covered with gold in the manner of a number of Tutankhamen's small figures. The face is finely carved in profile; the well-cut chin can be seen in detail where the gold has worn off. The body is slender with shoulders shown frontally, but the hips, and the legs which are only carved to the knees, turn towards the left. The left arm of the figure is bent across the body, as in numbers of the princesses' figures, and here holds a cornet-shaped bouquet sheath over the left shoulder. The upper right arm is beside the body but then reaches out from the skirt, as though holding something. The hand is missing and was evidently carved with whatever it held, because except for a splinter of raw reddish wood projecting from the top of the head and

71

43. Sketch of a wooden box lid from Tutankhamen's tomb with kilt on Amarna princess resembling the figures on plate 42 (Cairo).

[UC 24311]
Provenance: Qurneh, West Bank, Thebes; Amarna or Post-Amarna Period, c. 1379-1352 B.C. Wood, coated with *gesso* and gold. Height 7·3 cm. Width 3·0 cm. Lit. [1]W. M F. Petrie, *Objects of Daily Use*, p. 43 pl. XXXVIII (29), 1927. Comparisons: [2]H. Carter and A. C. Mace, *Tomb of Tutankhamen*, 1923-1933, Vol. I, pl. LXIII; [3]Vol. III, frontispiece; [4]Vol. III, p. 118; [5]It is worn by the small figure picking grapes on an ivory plaque in the Louvre (E.14,374), C. Desroches-Noblecourt, J.E.A. 54, pl. XIV, 1968; [6]C. Desroches-Noblecourt, *Tutankhamen*, p. 244, fig. 148, London, 1967.

obviously broken from the background, all the edges—at the wrist, top of the head and sheath, and at the knees—appear to have been finished; in most places where the gold has worn off, there are the remains of the white gesso under-coat. These surfaces were presumably fitted against other objects in an openwork or inlaid scene, as on much of Tutankhamen's furniture. Possibly lotuses were placed at the top of the sheath and perhaps a "sash", by the right hand. The piece is backed by a finely woven material under a red substance, probably adhesive (?).

The wig on this gold figure, although without the uraeus, is the same shape as worn by the Queen on the back of Tutankhamen's golden throne.[2] In itself this is no proof of the identity or sex of the epicene little figure; comparing it with others on an ivory lid from Tutankhamen's tomb shows it is not possible to determine people's sex in this period by what they wear.[3]

On the ivory lid, it is the King who wears a similar wig. He and the Queen stand facing each other above two small kneeling figures, picking flowers in a garden, described by Howard Carter as "Court maidens".[4] But one wears the wig, with a fillet, as this gold figure and the King above; she carries in her bent left arm a sheaf of flowers over her left shoulder. The other wears the long plaited wig, with the royal side-lock like the Queen above her. Both kneeling figures wear the *shendyt* kilt like the King, normally worn by men,[5] but there is a parallel for a princess wearing it on another box from the tomb, where Nefer-neferu-re, the second youngest princess, wears the same kilt.[6] Her named portrait, the small figures on the ivory lid, and this gold figure have enough likenesses and features in common to indicate that they are probably all portraits of the youngest Amarna princesses at the Theban Court.

There is no data as to where at Qurneh the gold figure came from. Scattered in the area around Tutankhamen's tomb were objects bearing his name; a bowl in the desert, and gold, with his name and that of Ankhesenamen and Ay on it in a rock-hewn chamber. Embalmers' equipment was found in the pit, with the flower necklace from a guest at the funeral banquet. This figure, too, could be an object from his Court; it has the *insouciant* grace of the young royal figures of the Amarna age.

STONE INLAYS

[UC 1. 314; 2. 295; 3. 316; 4. 304/312; 5. 296; 6. 310; 7. 260; 8. 326; 9. 122; 10. 128; 11. 271; 12. 123; 13. 263/64; 14. 194; 15. 307; 16. 279; 17. 24524; 18. 288; 19. 273; 20-22. 281/286/680] Provenance: Amarna. Limestone, sandstone, slate, quartzite, marble, diorite, a porous "pumice stone" and Egyptian alabaster, usually applied to calcite in Egyptian antiquities. The tall white reed, top centre. Height 11·5 cm. Width 3·5 cm. The small black reed, right of centre, bottom row. Height 3·5 cm. Width 0·5 cm. Lit. [1]P. *T/A*, pp. 11, 12. Unpublished.

On this plate are some of the many stone inlays which Petrie found; these had fallen from the walls, cornices and doorways of the buildings at Amarna which were destroyed and quarried for stone. They repeat in a variety of colours the glazed inlays which he described and drew in detail.[1] Limestone, he notes, was a favourite background for the inlays, which is understandable in view of the marble-smooth white surface they gave the finest pieces, which must have gleamed in the sunlight and made the multi-coloured inscriptions legible, and the scenes visible from afar. Red and black granite and diorite inlaid in the white background, black granite in yellow quartzite, white alabaster in red granite were some of the examples he found. The skill in carving the brittle stones was consummate. In small inscriptions, glass and obsidian were used for the slim lines, of which there are some examples in the Collection.

Bottom Row

In the bottom row, except for the smaller slate example of the wick of flax, *ḥ*[1], on the left of the central disk,[2] all the signs are of diorite; left is the goddess *M3't*,[3] and the larger *ḥ* sign;[4] in the centre, the disk is over the knot of rope from the base of a cartouche;[5] on the right of that is the reed sign;[6] the dark fragment second to the right has spaces for inlaid leaves (?), presumably of another colour,[7] and in the bottom right corner is a bunch of grapes,[8] more usually found in the bright blue glaze.

In the centre row, the fingers on the left,[9] and the hand from an inlaid figure[10] are of limestone and quartzite respectively. The disk and horns are limestone;[11] the beautifully carved foot from an inlaid figure is of quartzite[12] and the feet of a wader bird of sandstone.[13] On the left, above the fingers, are two slate claws (?), remaining inlaid in a porous pumice-like stone[14] and in the top left corner, the water sign is also slate.[15] The broken feather on its right is a slate-like stone,[16] and below it, the geometric sign is marble.[17] The large central reed is Egyptian alabaster,[18] like the broken shape in the top right corner which is perhaps the calyx of a large lotus design.[19] The cluster of three[20]–[22] small inlays between them are all of marble.

44. A variety of stone inlays from figures and hieroglyphic inscriptions. (H. 11·5 cm. to 3·5 cm.).

73

Glass

AMARNA PRINCESSES—RED MOULDED GLASS

Besides the technical interest of this early piece of glass moulded for inlay, its artistry has achieved a notable portrait of two of the Amarna princesses as children. They face right and their nude figures with arms around each other's shoulders convey their youthfulness. The left arm of the taller princess is missing and the legs are broken off at the knees.

As the piece is not included in Petrie's description of glass-making at Amarna, it is undoubtedly a more recent acquisition.' He wrote of polished glass, cut mouldings and engraved patterns and, in some unpublished notes, of glass being patted into strips for inlays and small figures; all these processes are evident in this piece. Its flat back and straight sides were apparently shaped in a mould, but the curves of the faces and bodies were probably modelled by hand. Narrow ribbon strips appear to have been applied for the princesses' hands on each other's shoulders and for their ears; the ear of the taller princess has a scratch in front of it from a tool (?). Delicate lines made within the forms, to finish shaping the bodies, were evidently engraved with a sharp edged tool while the material was still viscid.

A break across the middle of the figures has been joined and the original red of the glass can be seen in the fractures of the piece which is otherwise covered by a "bloom". Otherwise discolouration is limited to small patches of blue-black on the sides and back.

The delicacy of the inlay resembles the red glass figures of Tutankhamen and Ankhesenamen inlaid on the back of his golden throne, and it possibly came from a similarly elaborate scene. In sensitivity it is reminiscent of the Amarna princesses as children at the feet of their parents, in the Ashmolean mural from their house, and possibly it was part of a similar family group.

Facsimile of Plate V. See p. 64.

[UC 2235]
Provenance: Unknown. Amarna period. Opaque red (cuprous oxide) glass. Height 9·0 cm. Width 4·5 cm. Lit. J. Samson, *C/A III*, p. 228, pl. CVII (4). Comparisons: ¹P. *T/A*, pp. 25-27. Mural, Ashmolean Museum, Oxford, No. 1893.1. See, N. de G. Davies, *J.E.A.*, VII, frontispiece.

Plate 14b

SIX OBJECTS OF 'AMARNA' GLASS; plates 45 (i) and (ii).

1. *Hieroglyph h, (i) left: (overleaf).*

The wick of twisted flax is dark blue glass which can be seen dark and shiny in a crack at the side of it. Otherwise the front and particularly the less polished back has a "bloom" on it which also covers the break at the top and

[UC 302]
Provenance: Amarna. Glass. Height 5·0 cm. Width 1·5 cm. Unpublished.

bottom of the piece. It is an inlay with a flat back and shallow straight sides probably moulded. The twists of flax could have been applied in strips or may possibly have been shaped and divided by a tool while the glass was viscid.

45(i). Glass hieroglyph (H. 5 cm.) and red ear-rings.

2. *Red glass ear-rings, (i) right:*

The pair of opaque red (cuprous oxide) stud ear-rings show no sign of a join between the stud and the shank. The glass has only the faintest surface "bloom" which pales the colour and presumably, if there were a chip, the fuller brownish red would show underneath. The only evidence of decay besides the "bloom" is occasional faint green veining perceptible on the studs. There is no possibility, in this example, of the thick shank being attached to the stud by a thinner screw which could go more comfortably through a pierced ear-lobe; the shanks are approximately 0·8 centimetres in diameter near the end which is shaped (squeezed?) into a rough point.

[UC 22881]
Provenance: Amarna. Glass. Diameter of studs 2·0 cm. Length of shank 1·7 cm. Diameter 0·8 cm. Lit. J. Samson, *C/A III*, p. 228.

3. *Inlay head, (ii) top left: (overleaf).*

This remarkable inlay is of opaque red glass as can be seen in a small chip; otherwise the surface has decayed to an opaque chalky irridescence of pink and green. The piece has the flat back and straight upright sides of moulded glass; the back is roughened as though to help fix it to the background. The depth of the edge of the profile is 0·5 centimetres.

The inlay faces right. The eye and a line of the eyebrow are recessed for additional inlays. The line from the brow to the tip of the nose is at the angle usual in the princesses' profiles. The nostril is delicately modelled and at the inner corner of the mouth is the downward line seen in many Amarna portraits. The lips are thick, and they and the line between them, as well as the shape of the chin, are carried around the side as though to fit into a

[UC 22078] Head (overleaf)
Provenance: Unknown. Amarna style. Glass. Height 3·1 cm. Width 2·8 cm. Depth 0·6 cm. across the neck. Unpublished. Comparisons: E. Riefstahl, *AEG & G.*, Nos. 43 and 76, Brooklyn, 1969. H. Muller, *AKK & MAS*, p. 95, A 135.

precise outline prepared for the inlay. The nostril is only modelled on the surface. The modelling on the face would have risen from the background in *bas-relief*, with the head evidently meant to be placed into the background.

Up the back of the neck and face runs a thin vertical raised line to meet another raised line on a downward angle at the top of the face where the head-dress would be placed. The area between the raised lines is recessed. Two incised lines in the neck show the typical Amarna folds.

Plate 14b

The head and features are in the mature style of Amarna art. A composite inlay in glass made with such delicacy and precision suggests a royal head from a figure like those of Tutankhamen and his Queen on the back of his golden throne. Its appearance suggests an Amarna princess, perhaps from such a scene on royal furniture.

45(ii). Inlay head (H. 3·1 cm.), hieroglyphs and fragment of bowl.

[UC 305]
Provenance: Amarna. Glass. Length 2·2 cm. Width 0·5 cm. Unpublished.

[UC 12476]
Provenance: Amarna. Glass. Height 3·0 cm. Diameter 5·6 cm. Lit. P. *T/A*, pl. XIII, 36. W. M. F. Petrie, *Scarabs and Cylinders*, pl. XXXVI, 18, 10. (51), London, 1917.

[UC 289]
Provenance: Amarna. Glass. Height 2·2 cm. Width 4·4 cm. Unpublished. Comparison: P. *T/A*, pp. 25-28, pl. XIII.

4. *The N sign, (ii) top right:*
Part of the hieroglyph *n* is broken at both ends. It is opaque dark blue-black glass, now misted over with a "bloom" except in the fractures where the original dark depth of the colour shows.

5. *Fragment of blue glass vessel, (ii) bottom left:*
The opaque blue glass of this convex fragment from a vessel is completely covered by pale brown decay except for some chips around the broken edges where the light, bright blue shows. Inlaid white remains in the hieroglyphs of the earlier name of the Aten in the top part of two cartouches. On the left cartouche is *m rn.f m Šw n* (. . . .); on the right *Ḥr ȝḫt* (. . . .).

6. *Inlay hieroglyph, the sun's rays, (ii) bottom right:*
The surface of this opaque dark blue glass inlay is now covered by a pale chalky "bloom". It is part of the hieroglyph *ḥr*. The incised lines across the "hill" and forming the sun's rays are uneven, little more than scratched on, presumably when the glass was viscid.

Faience and Moulds

FAIENCE OBJECTS FROM THE COLLECTION

The term "faience" in this context is used to describe objects from Amarna made of quartz frit (powdered quartz) and then glazed. The few examples from the Collection shown here include separate inlays, glazed tiles with inlaid designs, amulets and seals.

Some fit into or closely resemble examples in the thousands of moulds brought back by Petrie from Amarna. Others show variations on the Amarna themes.

Lit. P. *T/A*, chap. II, p. 12; chap. IV, pp. 25-30, pls. XVI-XX. J. Samson, *C/A III*, pp. 228/229; pls. CVII (5-10); pl. CVIII (UC 2115, 1147, 1238, 1360, 722, 1258, 2038, 1106, 1114). Comparisons: *C/A*, Pt. I, II and III. E. Riefstahl, *Glass and Glazes from Ancient Egypt*, Brooklyn Museum, 1948 and *Ancient Egyptian Glass and Glazes*, Brooklyn Museum, 1969. H. W. Muller, *Ägyptische Kunstwerde, Kleinfunde und Glas*, Berlin, 1964. A. Lucas, *Ancient Egyptian Materials and Industries* (4th edition revised by J. R. Harris), London, 1962.

ANIMAL AMULETS AND RINGS

All 33 objects in these plates are faience animals; felines, birds, fish, reptiles and insects. The majority are amulets with threading holes. Others are ring bezels and inlays. Those without references to Petrie's *Tell el Amarna* are unpublished"

"Cats" (i)

In this row below are cats, large and small. On the extreme left, the seated cat has an intact threading hole fitted into the hollow at the back of the head. It is carved identically on both sides and was glazed back and front, but most of the colour has faded and worn to patches of pale green with the white composition showing between them. The cat facing right is seated on a base. The pose, upright ears and mask are typically feline.

[UC 23979]
Height 2·0 cm. Width 1·2 cm.

46(i). Faience "Cats".

To the right of it are three amulets of small indistinctly modelled, seated cats. Their bodies face right on a thin base, but their heads turn to the front. The threading hole is through the body of the central example and on the back of the right-hand cat, but broken. They are glazed front and back,

[UC 23680, 1213]
Height 0·8 cm.

blue, yellow and blue-green in that order. They are so small and roughly made that their significance may have been merely as pet kittens for children's amulets.

[UC 1189] (i)
Length 1·0 cm.

The animal second from the right is blurred by the covering of white glaze. It appears to be stalking on all fours, moving to the right. A fragment at the back is possibly part of a threading hole.

[UC 1211] (i)
Height 1·8 cm. Width 0·6 cm.

In the top right corner is a back view of a distinctly made figure of the goddess Sekhmet. It is glazed bright blue. The lioness-headed human figure faces forward and stands on a base. It is finely made. The ears are upright on the leonine head. Over the breasts are the lappets of a wig. The right arm hangs by the side, the left bends forward over the body to hold a papyrus sceptre to the front. There is a threading hole through the head. On the back are two parallel horizontal ridges shown on the plate.

46(ii). Ring bezels and fish amulets. (Tallest 1·7 cm.)

First Row (ii)

In the first row all the objects are ring bezels with remnants of the shanks behind. All the animals face right, except the calf in the broken bezel second to the left.

[UC 1030]
Diam. 1·5 cm. Lit. P. *T/A*, pl. XVI (185).

The bezel on the left is glazed yellow on both sides; it is oval with broken ends. The open-work design shows a frisking calf in the reeds, which Petrie noted was in the jewellery as well as on the painted floors in the central palace. The bovid has large ears and it gallops to the right with tail arched. A double line makes a feature of the rim.

[UC 23814]
Height 1·7 cm.

Next to it is the left side of an unusually deep broken bezel in apple green glaze. On it, a long-horned ibex (?) with a powerful neck, upright head and large curled horns is finely executed. Below it is a calf resting on one knee with the other raised; it faces left and it is apparently a suckling, taking its mother's milk. It has long ears, an upturned stump of a tail and the leggy gawkiness of a young animal.

[UC 1026]
Length 2·0 cm.

The centre bezel is a bright blue oval with straight ends. It is glazed blue both sides but the back, where the shank joined the bezel, is touched with brown. A long-horned ibex (?) prances right with lifted forelegs and the hind legs separated as though it were moving. The tail is short; the surrounding reeds are blurred.

[UC 2038]
Length 1·5 cm.

The broken bezel second right is glazed olive green both sides. In the open-work design a long-horned ibex (?) is lying with its legs bent under it.

78

The carving is perfectly formed in *bas-relief*, the horns carved well, in front of the notched top rim, and the flowing lines of the animal are unspoilt by the break in the bezel behind it.

On the right the bezel which is straight at the ends and perhaps meant to be at the top, is glazed yellow both sides. The ibex has long curved horns and a stumpy tail. The legs are bent and the rump of the animal raised as though it were moving fast. Below it is a shape of reeds (?).

Second Row

Of the fish in this row, two are amulets, one probably an inlay, and two are probably ring bezels.

On the left, the fish facing right is bright blue and glazed both sides. It is slightly convex and, although without the signs of a shank, was probably intended for a small ring bezel. It is very similar to the one on the right of the row which was thus intended. It resembles the *'int* or "bulti" fish. The head, tail and fins are shaped, and the nose, eyes and gills are incised. Petrie has a similar mould on Plate XVII (331) T/A.

Second on the left, the largest fish with the head missing is glazed white on the front and flat back and was possibly an inlay. The body is slightly convex on the obverse. The scales are stippled and the fins and tail striped. Two upward-curving lines are incised along the lower body from the break. The details are well executed.

The two slim fish resemble the *ẖȝt* of the Oxyrhynchus fish, and are both amulets. The centre one is glazed in bright blue all round, with the nose, fins and tail shaped and an intact threading hole at the head. The second example from the right is covered with faded pale blue glaze. The features of the fish are similar but less well defined. The threading hole on the nose is broken. Both are shown upside down. The "bulti"-type fish on the right is blue and resembles the one on the left of the row, but the features are blurred by poor glazing. It is definitely a ring bezel with traces of the shanks remaining. The head, tail and fins are shaped, the eye incised as a circle behind the nose. The body is striped and stippled.

[UC 2036]
Length 1·8 cm. P. *T/A*, pl. XVI (188).

[UC 1180]
Length 2·0 cm.

[UC 2061]
Length 2·4 cm. Width 2·0 cm.

Similar mould, P. *T/A*, pl. XVII (330)

[UC 2064, 1179]
Fish 1. Length 1·9 cm. Fish 2. Length 2·0 cm. P. *T/A*, pl. XVI (195).

Comparison: P. *T/A*, pl. XVII (332).

46(iii). Faience birds. (Tallest 1·5 cm.)

Birds (iii)

Left of the row above, with faded blue glaze on all surfaces is an amulet of the Horus falcon, facing right. It is characteristically shaped front and back. The wing feathers descend to the tail which rests on the base, as do the front legs; these are defined on both sides and a hole separates them from the body. The threading hole behind the head is intact.

Second left, the bird has worn green glaze on the front and flat back. The strong neck, long low body and sturdy legs suggest a duck or goose. The end tail feathers are missing, but it might be a white-fronted *gb*-goose from an inlaid inscription. It faces right; lines distinguish the wings and the legs.

Third left, the long-legged heron has green glaze both sides. It has the

[UC 23674]
Height 1·5 cm. Width 1·5 cm.
Similar mould, P. *T/A*, pl. XVII (314).

[UC 1215]
Length 1·3 cm. Height 1·5 cm.

head and crest, curved neck, body feathers and straight legs of the *šnty* heron and although so delicately made, may have been from an inscription. It also resembles the *bnw* phoenix. The eye is incised; the bird, facing right, stands on a base.

Third from the right, the bird is glazed green on the front and flat back, and it faces right. It was possibly the hieroglyph *wr* from an inscription, as it resembles the swallow or martin with the squared tail feathers. The glaze is worn on the front surface but shapes the wings and tail. The legs are bent and placed on a short base.

The flying bird second from the right is glazed on the front and flat back with a pale red. The head has a small blob on it but this is unlikely to be a threading hole and the piece was probably an inlay. The spread wings are striped with feathers, also suggested on the body and tail.

The ring bezel on the right has a worn blue glaze on all surfaces. A bird is fixed in an upright position in the centre, possibly a roughly shaped chick. There are traces at the back where the shank has broken off both sides. The raised shape fixed at right angles to the bezel must have made a clumsy ring and it is remarkable that such a frail fixture has remained in place.

Top Row (iv)

In the top row are six examples of the cobra, all of which had threading holes and are presumably amulets.

On the left, covered by a "peacock" or green-blue glaze, is a cobra with head and puffed neck, which is raised; the rest of the body is curled in horizontal rings behind it on a base. It faces right and the projection from the head is an intact threading hole.

Second left, the cobra is covered with a faded green glaze. It faces frontally. Down the body are raised V-shapes like the cloisons on ornate jewelled uraei.

Third left, the raised head and puffed-out neck of the cobra are in the same position. There was a threading hole at the back, now broken, and the green glaze covering the piece is faded. Below the head are the V-shaped cloisons of larger bejewelled examples. They are in the position of Akhenaten's name on the mould, left of the third row on Plate 49, which this faience amulet otherwise resembles. The head, eyes and mouth are distinctly modelled.

46(iv). Reptiles and insects. (Tallest 2·3 cm.)

Third from the right is an amulet of a twisting snake, glazed blue all over. The body is puffed-out below the head, but thins as it descends and twists back on itself. The eye is clearly marked. There is a broken threading hole behind the head.

In both the last two amulets on the right, the cobra has its head raised and body undulating against a background. Second from the right, the snake and background are glazed blue all over. The raised head and puffed-out body drops and then curls up and down on a base line and against the background from which there was a threading hole in the top, centre.

On the extreme right, the snake covered in faded green glass is in the same undulating position but the head is pushed forward and the body is not puffed out. The background is smaller and there is no base line. The threading hole at the top is intact.

Second Row

In the next row are four flies in different colours and materials, and on the right a small faience lizard. On the left is a black stone fly, well shaped, with a broken threading hole from its head.

The next two flies are well carved in carnelian and are very similar. The first has a complete threading hole from its head.

In the one in the centre of the plate, the threading hole is broken.

Second to the right, the fly amulet is glazed all over in pale red. The carving is detailed. The eyes bulge from the head, which, like the body, is striped. The wings are well modelled.

In the right corner, the faience lizard amulet is glazed green all over. It is shaped as the *ḥnt3sw*, perhaps for *'s3*—"many". From the long tapering body with the tail swung to one side, two legs are shown each side and the distinctly shaped head has a threading hole through it.

[UC 2148]
Length 1·5 cm. Width 0·6 cm.

[UC 1921]
Height 1·3 cm. Width 0·8 cm.

[UC 23644]
Height 1·5 cm. Width 1·2 cm.

[UC 1197]
Height 1·5 cm. Width 1·0 cm.

[UC 23664]
Length 1·2 cm. Width 0·7 cm.

[UC 23829]
Length 1·1 cm. Width 0·7 cm.

[UC 2132]
Length 1·7 cm. Width 1·1 cm.

[UC 1187]
Length 1·6 cm. Width 0·5 cm.

ROYAL AND RELIGIOUS FAIENCE AMULETS

The faience amulets in these plates show the retention of old ideas and beliefs by the people of Amarna where these amulets were made for them to wear. Few of them relate directly to Aten worship.

The amulet on the left below and next to it on the right are both crouching figures in the traditionally infantile pose of finger to mouth as shown in moulds in the middle row, Plate 49. Hayes thought these represented the King as a child of the Aten.[1] But the appearance of the left example is more like the traditional figure of the infant Horus, although the blue one on its right is unmistakably the King.

47(i). Symbolic figures. (Tallest 3·3 cm.)

[UC 1239]
Height 3·3 cm. Depth 0·5 cm.

[UC 1240]
Height 2·3 cm. Width 1·0 cm.

[UC 2008]
Height 2·0 cm. Width 1·0 cm.

[UC 1221]
Height 2·0 cm. Width 18·0 cm.

[UC 997, 2009]
Diam. at back 1·5 cm. Width 1·0 cm.

[UC 1247, 1244]
Height 1·5 cm. Width 0·7 cm.

[UC 1103]
Length 2·5 cm. Width 0·9 cm.

[UC 1377]
Height 2·2 cm.

[UC 1376]
Height 2·0 cm.

The larger example is glazed red overall and has an intact threading hole from the head. The figure is seated on a base, facing right with right hand on knee and left to lips. The glaze by the neck is blurred but appears to fall from the head in the side-lock worn by the infant Horus.

Second from the left the crouching figure of the King, hand to mouth, faces right. He wears the blue crown with a streamer down the back and the *shendyt* kilt. The amulet is glazed blue overall and the threading hole from the top of the head is intact. Hayes wrote of these openwork figures in the Metropolitan Museum as being only blue,[1] but there is a similar one in the Ashmolean Museum which is yellow glaze.

Third from the left the small, comparatively indistinct figure has a worn blue glaze, overall. The figure faces right with profile face and feet and frontal body. On the head is possibly a plumed head-dress, as the top projection is a broken threading hole; it has a leonine appearance, perhaps a mane, and the figure could be Bes, one of the most popular Amarna amulets, with left hand forward holding a gnarled stick and the right one behind him bending to his tail.

Fourth from the left, the small figure stands on a base against a background and faces right. It is covered with a blurred, pale blue glass-like glaze. The shape suggests a bearded King wearing the Crown of Lower Egypt and a kilt is suggested. The left hand holds a sceptre (?) in front; the right hangs down the back.

The two ovals third and fourth from the right are ring bezels with the remains of shanks behind them. The blurred design of the left example is explained by the one on its right. That on the left is glazed blue all over. In the openwork design, a small figure faces a tall shape on the right which it touches with the left hand, the right arm dropping behind the figure. The design is too indistinct to be self explanatory but interesting to compare with the parallel scene on the right. This bezel is glazed green back and front and has part of the shank remaining one side. In this the figure appears to be the Queen in a tall crown and either a clinging gown, or none, standing in the same pose in relation to a high floral decoration in a garden or perhaps a pavilion, as there are shapes hanging above, resembling bunches of grapes. The same overhead decor is on the plaque on the bottom right corner. The top edge of the green bezel is broken. Both bezels are the same size and were probably children's rings.

The last two amulets in the top row are both small naked figures striding to the right, against a background. On both the overall green glaze has faded. Both have an arm hanging before and behind the figure. There is a blurred wig (?) on the back of the heads.

First Row (ii)

Left of the first row, covered in dark, matt, purple glaze is the *tit*-amulet, found with those signifying life and welfare and sometimes connected with Isis. As they are often red, the glaze on this one has possibly darkened. It is chipped at the top but has an intact threading hole at the bottom.

The larger *hst*-vase third from the left is glazed bright blue and has the remains of a threading hole from the bottom, with possibly another at the top.

The smaller *hst*-vase in the centre is a dark purple vitreous glaze with faint pink showing in the irridescent surface. It has the remains of a threading hole top and bottom.

The *w3s*-sceptre is glazed bright blue overall and has a complete threading hole top and bottom.

Third from the right the wick of flax is glazed blue, overall, and has an intact threading hole at the top.

The *ʿankh* sign second from the right is glazed bright blue overall. Four threading holes were pierced through it front to back at the top, bottom and on both sides; the right hand one is now broken away.

The *nfr* sign on the right is completely glazed with blue, now faded. A threading hole remains at the top with a trace left of one at the bottom.

Bottom Row

Left of the bottom row is the *ʿankh* with arms both sides holding the edges of an enclosing *ḥb-sd* booth (?). This is broken at the top right corner. The amulet is glazed blue at front and back. One threading hole is intact in the bottom left-hand corner with the suggestion of the remains of another on the right and possibly one at the break on the left side.

Second left of the bottom row the *ḥb-sd* festival hall is glazed blue overall, with two complete threading holes at the top and a broken one at the centre bottom. The design is clear and detailed and has the diamond shape in the semi-circular base.

Third left and glazed blue overall is the phrase *mry 'Imn*. The hieroglyphs are against a background and, although an unexpected amulet for Amarna, it has a complete threading hole top and bottom.

Two of the very numerous *wd3t* eyes in the centre of the bottom row are both glazed blue overall. The one on the left has a *nfr* sign on the back; the other an *ʿankh*.

Second from the right, the amulet which is almost square is grey and gritty in texture, possibly unglazed. A bovine animal wearing plumes on its head is festooned as those shown in procession, possibly to be sacrificed for an Aten altar.[2] It is walking to the right. With the top threading hole, which is intact, it is perhaps a cow or bull with amuletic significance.

47(ii). Hieroglyphic amulets. (Tallest 3 cm.)

[UC 2102]
Length 3·0 cm.

[UC 1112]
Length 1·4 cm.

[UC 2093]
Length 1·8 cm.

[UC 1110]
Length 2·2 cm.

[UC 1108]
Length 1·5 cm. Width 1·2 cm.

[UC 1113]
Length 1·8 cm. Width 1·1 cm.

[UC 1107]
Length 1·9 cm. Width 0·9 cm.

[UC 24208, 1151]
Length 1·4 cm. and 1·5 cm.

[UC 2142]
Height 2·0 cm. Width 2·7 cm.

83

[UC 1016]

Width 1·5 cm. Height 1·3 cm. Comparisons: [1]W. C. Hayes, *Scepter of Egypt, II*, pp. 290-291, New York, 1968; [2]N. de G. Davies, *RTA*, I, pl. XIV, London, 1903; [3]J. D. Cooney, *Amarna Reliefs from Hermopolis in American Collections*, Nos. 38 and 39, Brooklyn Museum, 1965. G. Roeder, *Amarna Reliefs aus Hermopolis*, pl. 175, pl. 33, Hildesheim, 1969.

On the bottom right corner is a rectangular plaque broken at the left. It is glazed blue front and back, although, at the back, a horizontal strip across the centre remains unglazed, as though it had been mounted on a cross-bar. No trace of threading hole or shank remains. It resembles a scene in a manger, or perhaps a shrine. Facing right is the front of the body, the forelegs and head of a calf-like animal with large ears, a horn and long head. On its right facing it, a small standing figure reaches towards its mouth as though feeding it. Across the top of the enclosure is a row of decoration, apparently suspended (bunches of grapes?), which are met by points from a serrated edge at the top of the plaque; the right and bottom rims are plain. The open-work design is carefully wrought and placed, and although the feeding of a bovine animal in a manger is shown in Amarna reliefs from Hermopolis,[3] the decoration of this suggests a royal or religious enclosure.

FAIENCE SEALS (Plate 48 (i) - (iii) overleaf)

At the top of the plate are two half cylinder seals, either unfinished, or with the other half of each broken away. The outside of both is covered with a purple glaze not continued inside.

See Plate 50, top right mould

[UC 2031]
Length 2·0 cm. P. T/A, pl. XVI (182).

The horizontal open-work design on the left has a single rounded rim each end, from a mould. The design is horizontal; one bovine creature leaps to the right with head turned backwards and tail curled forward. Beneath it is a smaller, calf-like animal which springs to the left with tail outstretched. Petrie noted the parallel with the leaping calves on the palace painted pavements. Between and around the creatures is open-work design, strengthened by more solid shapes in the faience above and in front of the larger animal, but the piece is relatively fragile and possibly more decorative than useful.

[UC 2032]
Height 2·5 cm. P. T/A, pl. XVI (183).

The vertical seal on the right, also of violet glaze, is solid. There are three rounded rims at the top and two at the bottom edge. The vertical design is of a standing crowned god or king-like figure with a tall head-dress and skirt to the knees. His right hand is raised at the back of his head. He faces right and his left hand reaches out in front, perhaps to hold a sceptre or perhaps to touch an upright structure, possibly a tree (?). In front of this, the designs are more difficult to interpret but could be of an ibex below and perhaps a symbolic bird above. The design is not typically Egyptian in feeling and suggests Asiatic influence.

plates 48(i)
48(ii)

[UC 23662]
Length 1·6 cm.

The three scarabs in the second row and the four frogs beneath them are all seals with longitudinal threading holes.

On the left is the top half of an unglazed scarab with lines in the white composition marking the body and shaping the head. Half the threading hole remains.

[UC 1196]
Length 1·5 cm.

The central scarab is glazed bright green. The base is flat but uninscribed. The moulding and glazing is stylised and unusually poor.

[UC 1367]
Length 1·0 cm.

The smaller scarab bead on the right is glazed blue and has a roughly scratched six-point crossed design underneath.

Frog Seals (ii)

The four faience frog seals are remarkably finely made. See mould [UC 2125].

The seal on the left has a bright blue glaze and is modelled with meticulous detail. It shows tensely flexed legs and the back is striped by lines made in the glaze. The longitudinal hole emerges under its raised head. The animal is expertly wrought both artistically and anatomically. On the seal is the feather sign, *šwt*, Shu (?).

The frog second to the left is glazed dark blue with an unevenly incised six-pointed cross on the seal. Its frog-like pose, although similar, is less distinct than the frog on its left.

Second to the right, the frog seal is of a blue-grey glaze. It has stripes in the glaze down its back. Two protruding eyes appear to have been applied separately; they have a glass-like appearance of patchy bright green (decay?). On the seal is a *nefer* sign.

48(i). Purple glazed faience cylinder and flat seals in the shape of scarab beetles. (Tallest 2·5 cm.)

[UC 1177]
Length 1·0 cm.

[UC 23659]
Length 1·0 cm.

[UC 1176]
Length 1·0 cm. P. *T/A*, pl. XVII (329).

48(ii). Frog seals. (H. 1 cm.)

[UC 2127] (Plate 48(ii))
P. *T/A*, pl. XVII (328).

For comparison see E. Riefstahl,
A.E.G. and G., pl. 11, No. 25, Brooklyn Museum.

On the right, the particularly frog-like seal is glazed bright green with added brown eyes suffused with green below the brown suggesting glass and decay as in the example on the left. The threading hole emerges as on the others, under the head, but in this example the base is rounded in front making a platform under the hole which is between the flexed front legs. On the seal is the *šwt* feather, Shu (?).

48(iii). *Animal seals. (Longest 1·7 cm.)*

[UC 1203]
Length 1·7 cm.

[UC 1828]
Length 1·5 cm.

Animal Seals (iii)

The recumbent bovine creature on the left has a chalk-like grey-mauve glaze covering it, possibly once purple. The seal is uninscribed.

On the right is a clumsily-shaped scorpion on a base, perhaps for the purpose of a seal design, but left uninscribed. The design is confused by the thick glaze and further blurred by the threading hole which is across the head.

FAIENCE TILES AND INLAYS (See plate VI, p. 69)

Lit. P. *T/A*, pp. 27/28, paras. 61/2.
Comparisons: *City of Akhenaten*,
Parts I, II and III (two volumes).

The thirty-eight examples in this plate of faience inlays, and tiles with inlaid designs, are from typical Amarna scenes. They cover a range of techniques sometimes all used in the same piece. Besides those fallen from walls, columns and probably lintels and door jambs, some of the heavier tiles may have been in floor scenes and some of the smaller ones in furniture.

Top Row

[UC 412]
Width 10·0 cm. Lit. J. Samson, C/A
III, p. 228, pl. CVII (6).

On the heavy tile, top left, in which blue "water" lines and green lotus leaves are inlaid on a ground of white glaze, the edges of the lotus petals are incised, and their tips painted, brown. On the top right edge of the fragment part of a yellow inlay remains. The tile is heavy and a centimetre deep and suggests a floor tile. The back of it is unglazed.

[UC 542, 1279 and 1648]
Height 3·0 cm. to 3·5 cm. Depth
14·0 cm. to 15·0 cm. Lit. P. *T/A*,
pl. XIX, 481-488. Comparison: Muller,
A.K. K. & G., pl. 133.

On the three cornflowers in the top row centre the green calyxes and violet-blue petals are glazed front and back. The incised lines shaped on the calyx, and straight but fanning out for the petals, are only on the front. The right example is slightly convex and thicker than the other two. All appear to have been inlays.

[UC 1696]
Width 3·5 cm. Depth 1·0 cm.
Unpublished.

The fragment of cornflower on the second right, with incised green calyx and incised blue striped petals, is a smudgily glazed inlay with a flat back. The front is convex as though to project from a wall.

The tile on the top right corner has green leaves, and possibly a fruit (persea?) on the left, inlaid into a bluish-white ground. The veins of the leaves and fruit are painted brown, and the yellow stems edged with brown paint. The right edge of the tile is finished and shaped for inlaying. The back is shaped but unglazed.

Second Row

The triangular yellow fragment second left of the second row is from a bright yellow tile with an unusually high glaze. Spiky leaves of raised green glaze are edged with brown paint; the shapes of the stem and branch are incised on one side and outlined in brown on the other. The back is unglazed.

Third left of the second row the fragment has a small half-green flower, the white half possibly left unglazed; it is on a bluish-white ground. Olive green leaves and the stem are outlined in brown. This fragile delicate tile has a white glazed, curved top. The back is unglazed with grit adhering, possibly from a sandstone background.

Centre of the second line is the top curve of a thin, shaped tile. The finished top edge continues along the inward curve on the right, down to the break. The papyrus heads bend elegantly with the shape of the tile. The white background is smudged with brown, possibly from the paint with which the stamens are shown; the green heads of the flowers are also painted on but the green stems are inlaid. The back is unglazed, with the finished edges bevelled.

[UC 413]
Width 6·7 cm. Depth 1·0 cm. Lit. *Cat. Ancient Egyptian Art, Burlington Fine Art Club*, p. 31 (2), pl. XL, London, 1922.

[UC 452]
Width 4·5 cm. Unpublished.

[UC 24288]
Height 3·6 cm. Width 2·8 cm. Unpublished.

[UC 437]
Height 4·0 cm. Unpublished. Translation by Professor Fairman.

VI. *Fragments of faience tiles and inlays of fruit, flowers and from figures. Mosaic fragments in the bottom row. (Tallest H. 7 cm.).*

The rounded bunch of grapes second from the right is one of many such clusters of grapes of varying sizes. They are mostly glazed blue, although there are green ones. Some are flat at the back for inlay; others have a hole pierced through the top for use as a hanging decoration. This example is rounded, with two halves joined, but like many others, the top half of the back is cut away, presumably to fit against another shape.

[UC 23260]
Length 3·0 cm. Lit. P. T/A, pl. XIX (441-48).

The thin fragment of bright blue glaze below the grapes is a piece of glazed decorated surface, or a tile. The incised pattern could be a flower or part of an Aten ray and hand. The back is unglazed.

The papyrus head, on the right of the second row, is an unusual inlay. The head of the flower is thickened and glazed at the top, to stand out from a surface. It fans out from the bottom, deepening from the middle to half a centimetre in depth at the top. Incised lines ridge the green glaze, following the shape from top to bottom, with brown dots painted at the top. The top edge is finely finished with a glossy red-brown glaze. The back is unglazed, except for an overlapping green rim, formed around the unbroken edges from the front green glaze. This colour is also smudged into the red-brown top.

The fragment of convex lotus below the papyrus is a raised flower of coarse glaze work. The leaves are glazed green; the petals of blue-white are tipped with dots of dark blue glaze. The back is glazed white, blue-green, and at the top a thick yellow layer. It would project if inlaid.

Third Row

The fragment of "daisy" tile, on the left of the second row, is one of many similar tiles found by Petrie from the walls of the "Coronation" Hall of the central palace. This fragment has the coarse, gritty, green glaze which is typical of them, with the unglazed recessed circles for the white daisy inlays, and the unglazed back. Between the inlays blue flowers with black edges are painted on the surface. In this fragment they have raised yellow glazed centres and brown painted stems. The top edge is finished for inlaying. A broken white daisy with yellow centre is laid into the left recess.

The two kneeling figures in the third row are bound foreigners. On the left is a blue glazed figure of a kneeling Asiatic (?) and on the right a red glazed figure of a kneeling Nubian. Possibly they are both inlays from furniture, as both figures are flat at the back which is glazed.

In the centre of the third row is part of a red glazed royal hand. This perfectly fashioned and highly glazed piece suggests a scene in which a royal figure is offering to the Aten or conferring honours on a courtier. The thumb and three fingers are raised in *bas-relief* against a ground of the red tile, which is as highly glazed as the fingers except for the spaces between them where the surface is matt. The nails are separately added in white glaze. On the thumb the nail is but a white strip. Behind the thumb the top surface of the tile is a centimetre thick and highly glazed. At the tip of the thumb the highly glazed edge turns down and continues obliquely to the break below it. The back of the tile is also glazed but with a less high finish and it is cross hatched presumably to increase the purchase on a wall; gritty sand adheres to it, perhaps from a sandstone wall.

Right of the central inlay are three red glazed hands. The two flat, smaller hands are probably inlays of Aten hands from the ends of inlaid rays. They are glazed on the flat back, and at the wrists for placing them beside the adjacent shape. The top hand with traces of white now between the fingers is deeper and more rounded. It is glazed overall and suggests the hand of a princess.

The two red glazed poppy petals for inlay on the right of the third row are both glazed at the back. They are decorated with different techniques.

The left one has the black tip painted on it and the white dots inlaid; the right has the part of a circle inlaid with white glaze.

Fourth Row

The triangular red tile, left of the fourth row, is a background inlay tile with a slightly raised green bud inlaid in the centre. It is one of those described by Petrie as making a garland of flowers and buds on a red ground. The base is broken; the back is glazed.

[UC 899]
Height 6·0 cm. P. *T/A*, p. 28, para. 61, pl. XIX (487).

The fragment of lotus inlay tile, second left of the fourth row is, like the other tile, an example of a colourful lotus pattern on a red ground. In this the inlaid green leaves of the flower surround the diamond-shaped white petal which is tipped with purple-blue; the red background is left only in the one inverted triangle visible at the top edge. The back is unglazed.

[UC 1559]
Height 6·0 cm. Comparison with one from a house, *C/A II*, p. 21 (26/286), pl. XXX (3).

The small red triangular tile, third left, is another from a garland against a red ground. The green lotus bud tipped with yellow glaze at the base is inlaid in the centre of the triangle, and at the top of the bud blue glaze is inlaid in a line on the left. Where they occur there are usually two of these inlaid lines dividing the calyx, in recesses made by raised lines in the mould. The back is glazed.

[UC 1553]
Height 3·5 cm. P. *T/A*, pl. XIX (487).

The fragment of tile inlaid with blue flowers in the centre has a bluish-white ground. Both the blue flowers (cornflowers?) and the green stems are inlaid and empty shapes show where other inlays have been dislodged. The back is unglazed.

[UC 24289]
Width 3·5 cm. Unpublished.

On the lotus tile, second right of the fourth row, the inlaid green glazed leaves are slightly raised. They spring from a yellow glazed base. The petals are part of the white ground, their shapes being incised. They are slightly "brushed" with blue around the edges, against a white ground. The edges of the tile are glazed. On the unglazed back are two small rectangular mortises and the remains of a third for inlaying and fitting this tile into a scene.

[UC 908]
Height 7·0 cm. Muller, *A.K.K.* & G. pl. 125 c.

Right of the row is the edge of a tile on which the base is painted with dark brown to represent Nile mud (?). It has the trunk of a palm tree rising from it, painted red with brown painted spikes. Trace of brown painted leaves (?) show in the top right corner. The right edge of the tile is finished.

[UC 790]
Height 5·2 cm. Unpublished.

Bottom Row

Left of the bottom row are two "blue" crowns for inlays on the King's head, their size suggesting they come from a multi-coloured composite figure inlaid in furniture. They both have the shaped edge (at the bottom of the plate) for round the face, and the ridge across the crown. Both have incised circles and both are a pale lilac-blue glaze resembling the colour of two of Nefertiti's crowns in the Collection, one of which is an inlay. There are stone reliefs with spaces for the inlays of crowns, wigs, flowers and the sun's disk, and faience shapes for inlaying them in the Collection: but of any delicate inlaid furniture at Amarna only such fragmentary pieces as these remain, for which Tutankhamen's furniture offers a parallel.

[UC 1558, 1251]
Height 3·0 cm. and 1·0 cm. Comparisons: *C/A I*, p. 121, pl. XXXIV (1) and (2). Similar crown, *C/A II*, pl. XXVIII (6).

The red glazed inscription, bottom row, third left, is a thin fragment of surface from a dark red glazed tile. It is rough at the back. Part of the disk (?) is above the ʿankh; a vertical column line is on the right, and two lines at right angles on the bottom left. The lower finished edge is part of a circle.

[UC 23690]
Height 3·0 cm. Unpublished.

Three fragments of red glaze in the centre of the bottom row are inlaid

[UC 683, 685 and 687]
Width 6·0 cm. to 2·6 cm. Unpublished. Comparison: Muller, *A.K.K. & G.* pl. 199a and 199b.

[UC 607]
Width 2·0 cm. Unpublished.

[UC 1636, 1783 and 2139]
Width 3·5 cm. to 1·5 cm. P. *T/A*, pl. XVII (304, 307, 309).

[UC 419A, 420, 421]
Width 4·5 cm. to 4·0 cm. Unpublished.

[UC 472]
From nose to break, length 6·7 cm. From the back fin, width 6·2 cm. Unpublished.

with uneven yellow rhomboids and solid blue diamond shapes. The top two fragments are glazed red on both sides. Both are glazed at the back, the longer one with red, the shorter one with white. They could be part of the head and body of a snake for inlaying in a scene. The head shape is 1·2 centimetres deep; the shorter piece is 0·7 centimetres deep. The larger piece below them is broken on all edges, and suggests part of a cushion or footstool in an inlaid scene resembling the background to the two princesses in the Ashmolean mural from their home. It is only glazed on the surface, the back being rough or broken red tile.

The fragment of coloured mosaic in the bottom row, second right, is inlaid with a dark blue triangular network, itself inlaid with white circles; the "ground" of the tile appears to be equally small red inlays. In the top left corner is part of a turquoise diamond-shaped inlay; on the top right corner is half a similar diamond-shaped cavity. The piece could be from a foreigner's robe, and heralds the later inlaid shapes of mediaeval mosaics.

The three animal "offerings" on the bottom right corner are of a bovine head, trussed animal body, and the leg and foot of an animal, all in blue glaze. They are presumably from an inlaid scene of Aten offerings. The features on the head are painted brown.

FRAGMENTS OF FAIENCE TILES FROM POOL SCENES

The fifteen pieces of inlay in this plate show a variety of the techniques used in faience tiles at Amarna. The methods include varying the thickness of the glaze in shaping the pattern, as in the smaller of the two fish tiles; the use of "colour perspective" on the duck; and by supplementing inlaid pattern with painted and incised surface decoration on most of the fragments.

The subjects are reminiscent of the painted pavements, with fish and flowers in the pools, and fowl in the surrounding papyrus and reed plants. The tiles of reeds on the lower right of the plate are angled and shaped, presumably to fit around a central theme and maintain a flowing design without carrying the inlaid pattern over onto the next tile.

Bottom Row

All three tiles of water pattern left of the bottom row have a different colour scheme. The left example has dark blue water signs inlaid on pale blue glaze. It has a straight finished edge on the left.

The middle fragment has darker blue water signs laid into a white ground with the central yellow lotus base inlaid. The right edge is finished.

On the right fragment the water signs are alternate dark and light blue inlays with a dark brown edge, Nile mud (?) on the left.

Fish Tiles

Of the two fish tiles above the bottom row, the larger is a centimetre thick. It is of an unusually fine and smooth stone-like texture, with a thin glaze; this covers it, but the back is matt. The tile is broken perpendicularly from behind the back fin, which is chipped. The two curved brown lines from the bottom edge, gills (?), are deeply incised in the glaze and surface painted. The loop at the break and the stroke to the top like the line around the top are surface painted in brown. The eye is ringed with brown surface paint; the socket is recessed and glazed dark blue, with a raised brown glazed dot for the pupil; the mouth is realistically shaped as just open, by deep incision in the glaze, unpainted.

The smaller fish is only half the depth of the larger. The especially vitreous quality of the glaze covering it and the varied methods used on this tile give the fish a realistically underwater appearance. The fins and scales are painted brown. The folds around the eye are painted brown but also shaped by raised rings of glaze giving an effect of flesh. The eye is both painted and shaped. It is ringed with brown surface paint; the yellow glazed eyeball is raised, and an incised line surrounds the brown pupil. The stippling under the eye is of brown painted dots. The mouth is indicated both by incision and painting. The piece is glazed top and bottom but not at the back. The break cuts the tile behind the underneath front fin. A side fin is realistically painted on.

[UC 476]
Length 5·0 cm. Width 4·0 cm.
Unpublished.
Comparison: Muller, *A.K.K.* & *G.*, A, 122a, 122b.

VII. *Coloured faience tiles, a duck, fish and reeds from pool scenes.* (Tallest H. 7·9 cm.).

Second Row

On the head and body of the duck, second from the top on the left of the plate, the beak is broken, and only the front half of the bird remains. On it is an example of colour perspective by the use of warm and cool colours. The yellow wing is a slightly thicker glaze than the grey-blue breast feathers and is separated from them by an incised line, but the raised effect of the wing is largely from the use of the warm yellow over the cool blue. The body feathers are painted in brown and the eye is painted. The head feathers are also painted, but they are rippled, presumably by dragging the viscous glaze. A blue-white glaze covers the edges, but the back is thickened by a deposit, apparently from the background into which it was set.

[UC 509]
Height 4·3 cm. Width 4·3 cm.
Lit. *Cat. Ancient Egyptian Art, Burlington Fine Arts Club,* p. 31, pl. XL (g), London, 1922.

Top Row

The edge of the fragment of tile on the top left is slightly curved. All the

[UC 24287]
Width 3·7 cm. Unpublished.

[UC 483]
Width 3·5 cm. Unpublished.

[UCC 425]
Height 4·0 cm. Unpublished.

[UC 435]
Width 4·0 cm. Unpublished.

[UC 438A]
Width 3·2 cm. Unpublished.

[UC 445]
Width 2·5 cm. Unpublished.

[UC 424]
Height 5·0 cm. Lit. *Cat. Ancient Egyptian Art, Burlington Fine Arts Club*, pl. XL (h), London, 1922.

[UC 423]
Height 6·0 cm. Unpublished.

[UC 426]
Height 7·9 cm. Unpublished.

pattern, the green papyrus head reaching to the edge, its brown calyx, and the dots around the edge are painted on blue-white ground. The back is whitened and has a bevelled edge at the top for inlaying.

The fragment, second right of the top line, has a glazed slightly curved top edge. The green leaves are inlaid into the blue-white ground but the brown grass (?) between the leaves is painted on. The back is unglazed with a bevelled edge for in-fitting.

On the top right is a nearly square fragment of thick corner tile, with a finished top and right edge. The green leaves are inlaid and the brown decoration painted. The back is rough and unglazed, but the blue-white ground from the front partly covers the sides.

Second Row

The fragment of tile on the left of the second row is broken all round, but the base of the flower at the top and the hollow for another on the left show the techniques were varied. The green base of the flower and the red-brown calyx and the green stems are all inlaid. The brown outline of the stems is painted in grooves at the side of the inlaid green strip. The unexplained brown line left of the top flower is painted decoration, perhaps one of the rare examples of a misplaced stroke. The white ground is recessed where the flower is missing on the left. The back is thinly glazed with white.

The small fragment with stems on its right, the second row, is broken all round. It has two inlaid green stems outlined in brown. Between them another is outlined in brown without the inlaid green strip. On the left are two painted brown "spear" leaves. The background is a blue-white. The back is unglazed.

The small fragment of tile with leaves and flowers on the right has all edges broken except the top. The green leaves are inlaid but all the brown decoration surface painted. The top edge is bevelled for inlaying at the back, which has been glazed white.

Third Row

The two triangular pieces of reed tiles, in the third row, are an unusual shape. In the smaller, central, triangular fragment there is a finished edge on the left which is angled to the right, possibly to a point like the piece on its right. The green stems and flower heads are inlaid but the stamens painted on the surface. The back is glazed a blue-white.

The larger triangular tile on the right-hand side is clearly shaped for inlaying as a triangle. The back is unglazed, with one edge bevelled and one cut or moulded straight. The green flowers and stems are inlaid; the brown outlines are incised and painted and the stamens only surface painted. The ground is a greyish colour, possibly discoloured like the tile in the right corner. The back glaze is also a greyish white.

Bottom Row

The tile with a finished base-line in the bottom right corner has another finished edge turning up on the right, to the break. The back is unglazed. Both finished edges and the unglazed back have a grey gritty substance adhering. The background is an off-white, pearl-like glaze, perhaps from undue heat, as the back and broken right edge of the tile have been burnt. All the green stems are inlaid, but the red-brown basal sheath is painted on the surface.

NOTE ON AMARNA MOULDS

In Petrie's description of the thousands of red clay moulds he brought back from Amarna he writes that he rejected large quantities of the commonest, but amongst the hundreds in the Collection are many variations for the innumerable faience inlays and amulets. In some a part of the unglazed composition base remains; in others the colouring of the object made in them can still be seen. A number, especially where the design is small or the recess deep have a line across the edge of the clay to give more purchase when prising out the small "positive". In many the thumb and finger marks are left in the clay from its shaping when damp. Apart from the technical interest of how the intricate tiles and *minutiae* were made, there is information to be gained from the moulds which supplements that from the amulets; they also show the figures of the gods that were made for the populace alongside the Aten symbols. The small selection here shows some unexpected designs, and demonstrates, notably in the seals, contact with the Near East and the Aegean.

Where moulds are published by Petrie in *Tell el-Amarna* a reference is given; otherwise most are unpublished.

Plate VIII

Lit. P. *T/A*, pp. 25-30, pls. XIV to **XX**. Comparisons: *City of Akhenaten*, Vol. 1, p. 170, pl. XIII; Vol. II, pp. 114-117; pl. XLIX; Vol. III, p. 182, pl. C.

Facsimile of Colour Plate VIII. See p. 69.

Lit. P. *T/A*, p. 28, pl. XIX.

MOULDS WITH RELEVANT FAIENCE OBJECTS

The four moulds in this plate with relevant faience examples show various ways of making glazed tiles. At the top, the triangular mould has the shape of a lotus bud raised in the centre. This is for a tile similar to the one on its right, with the green bud set into the hollow made by the raised shape in the mould. The colour remains in many of the moulds where the red tiles were made as backgrounds for the coloured lotus garlands set into them. There are examples of the separate white petals and green faience lotus buds and leaves in the Collection, as well as moulds in which they were made.

The mould on the bottom left for an inlay of a cornflower has a faience example above it. Of the two lotus moulds, the bottom right is an example of a raised pattern, the other is recessed; above them are two inlaid lotus designs.

Red colouring remains in the triangular mould with a raised central bud on the top left of the plate. The red faience tile beside it has a green bud inlaid, in a hollow made by a similar mould. The green bud has two inlaid blue lines at the tip, making a point and suggesting the divisions in the calyx. The basal tip is painted yellow. The tile is glazed front and back.

The mould for a separate cornflower inlay, on the bottom left of the plate, could have made the faience example above it. The recess of the mould is 4·3 centimetres and it has the incisions for the usual shapes on the calyx and lines for the petals of the flower. The faience example is 4 centimetres long and shows the moulded markings on the green glazed calyx and violet petals.

The mould with a raised lotus design, bottom right of the plate, is for the typical lotus tile. The raised pattern has three outer leaves, at the centre and at each side; they run from the top to the raised elliptical base at the bottom.

[UC 1711, 1712]
Recess in mould, height 6·3 cm. Tile height 6·0 cm. Lit. P. *T/A*, pl. XIX (459). Comparison: Muller, *A.K.K. & G.*, Bud, pl. 133.

[UC 1647, 23637]
Lit. P. *T/A*, pl. XIX (481)(2). Comparison: Muller, *A.K.K. & G.*, pl. 133.

[UC 1710, 885]
Mould recess, height 4·8 cm. Faience
lotus, height 6·0 cm. Lit. P. T/A,
pl. XIX (458). Comparison: Muller,
A.K.K. & G., A, 125a, 125b, 126b.

[UC 1713]
Lotus recess, width 3·0 cm. Unpublished.

[UC 1715]
Width 3·3 cm. Lit. P. T/A, pl. XIX
(456).

The three petals each side of the central leaf are also raised.

In the faience example on its right, the three full length green outer leaves are inlaid in the hollows left by such a mould; one long diamond-shaped blue petal is inlaid each side of the central leaf, with a yellow diamond-shaped petal on each side of it. The ground is white. The yellow base is also inlaid in the hollow made by the mould

The centre mould with a recessed lotus design with three green leaves and a base has the usual number of three petals each side of the central leaf. The faience "positive" would have the lotus design raised from the background.

In the centre of the second row the small lotus-design spacer is a stylised example of three inlaid leaves, with one petal each side of the centre, and an inlaid base. All the inlays are purple in the white ground. At the back of the spacer there is a ridge across the top with five holes for the threads from a necklace, with another at the point of the spacer for them to be gathered through and presumably knotted.

MOULDS OF ROYAL AND RELIGIOUS SYMBOLS

49. Red clay moulds for faience amulets of royal and religious symbols. (Tallest H. 4 cm.).

[UC 2021]
Height 1·0 cm. to 1·2 cm.

[UC 2028]
Height 1·5 cm. P. T/A, pl. XVII (251, 250 and 254).

The nine moulds in this plate are of amuletic symbols with royal or religious significance.

Top Row

Left of the top row, the design is of two *nfr* signs pendant from the *wdȝt* eye. Beside it, in the centre, are three *nfr* signs from two eyes aligned as though in a face. Right of the top row, three ʿ*ankh* signs are pendant from the disk which has a raised uraeus in the centre.

94

Centre Row

The mould on the left and in the centre of the second row are both of a figure in the infantile position with knees drawn up and finger to mouth. The figure on the left, surrounded by a rectangle, faces right. It wears the *shendyt* kilt, and the side-lock of youth apparently over a shaven head. In the centre, facing left, is the small crouching figure of the King. He wears the blue crown with the uraeus in front and streamers behind, a necklace and the *shendyt* kilt. Hayes wrote of these designs possibly representing the King as "child of the Aten" and notes that in the Metropolitan Museum, the faience examples are only glazed blue. In this Collection, there is a red and blue faience figure in this pose. In the Ashmolean Museum, there is a similar small figure, glazed yellow.

Right of the second row is a naked, babyish figure facing right. It has a large head and bent legs.

Left of the third and bottom row is a cobra raised to strike. It is incised in detail. The body is moulded in depth and suggests it was for a faience cornice, perhaps on furniture, rather than to wear. The eyes and mouth are clearly modelled, and it has the V-shaped pattern on the body like the cloisons on bejewelled uraei. Above this pattern and below the head is a cartouche with the King's *pre-nomen Nfr-ḫprw-r̓ ı̓w -n-r̓* . The amulet of this form to be worn is without the inscription.

Bottom Row

In the centre of the bottom row is an enthroned queenly figure facing left. She holds the papyrus sceptre before her and what is probably the ῾*ankh* in her right hand near her knee. A diadem surmounts the vulture head-dress, reminiscent of the God's Wife of Amen assumed by royal heiresses in the XVIIIth Dynasty and her left breast is bare over her sheath-like dress. Although without a surmounting head-dress, the figure also suggests a link with Hathor.

Right of the third row is the most precisely detailed of all the Amarna moulds. On the head of the cat goddess Bast, and between her upright ears, is the disk with uraeus in the centre. A lappet each side of her neck covers part of the deep, ornamental collar she wears; this forms the top of the *menat* symbol that is continued below it in the usual shape and highly decorated.

MOULDS FOR A CROWN, A SEAL AND FIGURES OF GODS

Top Row

On the top left corner is a mould for Nefertiti's crown. It has the straight front line to rise from the Queen's brow and the flap which lies over the cap-band in front of her ear. The surface is covered with blue circles with a dot in the centre as on the King's blue crown.

The same decoration is on two faience examples in the Collection, of the Queen's tall crown, both of which are glazed a bluish-grey. One has a flat back and straight sides, probably moulded for an inlay.

The other is slightly curved as though from a composite statuette.

[UC 2003]
Height 2·0 cm.

[UC 2004]
Height 2·0 cm. P. *T/A*, pl. XVII (271 and 272). W. C. Hayes, *Scepter of Egypt*, *II*, pp. 290, 291, N.Y., 1968.

[UC 2006]
Height 1·4 cm.
P. *T/A*, pl. XVII (275).

[UC 2177]
Height 2·5 cm. Depth 0·5 cm.
P. *T/A*, pl. XVII (319).

[UC 2016]
Height 3·0 cm. Width 1·5 cm.
Lit. P. *T/A*, pl. XVII (284).

[UC 24312]
Height 2·7 cm. Unpublished.

[UC 2050]
Height 1·2 cm. Width 1·4 cm.
P. *T/A*, pl. XVII (258).

[UC 24271]
Width 2·5 cm.
[UC 24270]
Diameter 4·0 cm.
Two glazed war crowns are on colour plate VI

95

50. *Moulds with the plasticine 'positives' of a crown, a cylinder seal and five gods.* (*Tallest H. 3 cm.*).

[UC 2133]
Length 2·5 cm. Width 1·4 cm.
P. *T/A*, pl. XVI (181). Comparison:
C/A III, pl. LXXXIII (154)

[UC 2014]
Height 1·5 cm. Width 1·2 cm.
P. *T/A*, pl. XVII (276).

[UC 24335]
Height 2·7 cm. Width 2·0 cm.
P. *T/A*, pl. XVII (295).

Top right is a semi-circular mould for half a cylinder seal. The design is of an ibex (?) facing left; it stands on its hind legs with forelegs resting on the branches of a tree from which it seems about to nibble. The animal has strong curved horns, a large ear and a short, upturned, stumpy tail. It is clearly shown as male. The mould has a ridge top and bottom of the design, the latter forming the line on which the animal stands. The faience example, top left of plate 48, has a rounded rim each end, which would be made by this shape mould, and both are designs with foreign attributes.

Second Row

Left of the second row is the profile head and shoulder of a figure facing left. The eye and eyebrow, prominent nose and the mouth are clearly shown. The ear is large, and the long straight wig which falls front and back of the shoulder to the end of the design, is as though it were tucked behind it. Over the rounded shoulder, the rows of a large collar are incised; this is not shown in the drawing of an otherwise similar mould by Petrie. The mould has been blackened by smoke.

Centre of the second row is a two-sided creature with identical profile of head, body and foot facing each side. There is a fragmentary bright blue faience example in the Collection which fits into the double feet and lower part of the body, although the detailed design on the body is different. The head consists of a stylised long crocodile-like jaw with a circle and a central dot for the eye and nostril, joined by a line. Teeth are shaped in the open jaws. The body is covered by decoration between four upward curving lines which, with the shape of the body, widen as they descend. In the top and

96

bottom rows are circles with dots in the centre; the middle row has parallel upward stripes swinging outwards at the sides and these are echoed in the ribs of the large, flat, out-turned feet.

Right of the second row is a two-headed bovine animal or a presentation of two animals with heads in opposite directions. On the heads are horns and long ears and below the head two legs, presumably the front ones. Across edges of the mould is a horizontal line usually for prising out the faience shape, in this case possibly to preserve the heads of the very small design.

Bottom Row

Left of the bottom row is the mould of a seated animal facing left. It has long crocodile jaws, a prominent bulging eye high on its head, and a leonine mane behind big ears and over the front and back of the shoulders. A powerful rump is incised with lines suggesting fur or hair and the squatting pose with two forefeet in front is feline. There is a suggestion of Am-Mit in the expectantly open jaws of the creature and its compound characteristics.

Right of the bottom row, an animal facing left has the enlarged abdomen of Tauert, but the effect is less benign. The jaws are like a crocodile, and the shape with the projecting spine resembles hippopotamus goddesses with crocodile heads. A network of lines crosses the body and oblique stripes cross the perpendicular line down the projecting spine which ends in a tail above the back foot. Two flat feet are shown turning outward in a frontal view. A shape for the threading hole rises from the head.

[UC 2136]
Height 1·0 cm. Width 1·3 cm.
P. *T/A*, pl. XVII (306).

[UC 2159]
Height 3·0 cm. Width 1·8 cm.
P. *T/A*, pl. XVII (300).

[UC 2157]
Height 3·0 cm. Width 1·7 cm.
P. *T/A*, pl. XVII (296). Comparison: Budge, *From Fetish to God in Ancient Egypt*, p. 86, London, 1934.

Inscriptions

LIMESTONE SCARAB OF AMENOPHIS IV

This ceremonial scarab resembles in size and style those issued by Amenophis III to commemorate certain events, but in complete contrast, its content is religious. On it, Akhenaten as a young king faces right. He is seated on his right leg with his left knee raised and his arms uplifted to what were two large Aten cartouches, in the pose of the god Shu upholding the disk. The King wears a uraeus on his "bag" wig and under his right shoulder is part of

51a. Limestone scarab of Akhenaten as Amenophis IV. (L. 7 cm.).

98

the streamer from it. His necklace is a stylised semi-circle. The *shendyt* kilt is carved on the figure, below which is a large *nb* sign stretching nearly the width of the scarab. In front of him is a cartouche with his *pre-nomen*, and behind him his early throne name in another cartouche.

On the under surface, the left edge, part of the right edge and all the top of the scarab is chipped away. The damage is mostly to the surface stone, the top half taking most of the Aten names. Of the left Aten cartouche, only the bottom right corner remains with the reed and disk from the Aten name. At the base of the right cartouche the *3ḫt* is intact; level with this on the right are fragments of *nb pt*, at the end of a column of inscription.

The design is a striking parallel to that on the alabaster stela of the same scale in Berlin, where the Aten names are complete and in the early form. The significant difference is that, unlike the stela where the King is called Akhenaten, on the scarab his early name—*'Imn-ḥtp nṯr ḥḳ3 w3s*—Amenhotep, ruler of Thebes, is in the cartouche behind him. This has been rubbed to an ivory smooth concavity, presumably in an attempt to erase the association with Amen, as no damage has been done to his pre-nomen—*nfr-ḫprw-rˁ wˁ-n-rˁ*—in the cartouche in front of him. On the Berlin stela, Nefertiti's cartouche follows his name behind him where the scarab is broken away

[UC 2233]
Early Amarna period. Limestone. Length 7·0 cm. Width 5·0 cm. Lit. W. M. F. Petrie, *Scarabs and Cylinders with Names*, p. 27, pl. XXXVI (1), London, 1917. Comparison: *Catalogue Agyptisches Museum*, Berlin, p. 67, pl. 745, Inv. No. 2045.

51b. The head, back and legs of the scarab beetle on plate 51a. (L. 7 cm.).

but where there would have been room for it.

The carapace of the beetle is carved in detail; the eye is emphasised and the legs striated. A hole is bored longitudinally through it.

In 1917, Petrie included this scarab in his book *Scarabs and Cylinders*, but he gives no provenance for it. Presumably it was bought, but use of the King's early name suggests Thebes.

QUEEN TY'S SEAL

On the under surface of this limestone seal the central cartouche enclosing the royal name "Ty" is flanked on both sides with a spirited horse surmounted by a lizard—*ˁ3 sšmwt* (?). The carving is life-like and deep. The whole carved area is surrounded by an oval line. On the reverse the stone is roughly hewn into a raised spine which, although clumsy, would help to grasp the seal when

[UC 376]
Provenance: Amarna. Limestone. Length 16·5 cm. Width 6·5 cm. Depth 6·0 cm. J. Samson, *CA III*, an impression on pl. CVIII.

52. A seal for making a clay impression with Queen Ty's name in the centre and the signs for many horses either side. (L. 16·5 cm.).

stamping the imprint. Since the inscription describes Queen Ty, as "rich in horses", this seal could belong to the time of her visit to Amarna in year 12 and have been used to seal the wet mud clamped on the bolts of her stables. The deep cutting leaves a bold impression of raised shapes in *bas-relief*, resembling those on the mud sealings of the outermost door of Tutankhamen's tomb.

A CARVING OF PART OF THE EARLY ATEN NAME

[UC 069]
Amarna. Chalky limestone. Height 8·0 cm. Width 6·0 cm. Unpublished.

The carving of "*Re-Harakhty lives*" from the name of the Aten used before year 9, is in shallow sunk relief (*en creux*) with ornate surface detail. In the groove made for the surrounding rope of the cartouche are faint traces of red from the thin rods of faience once inlaid. There are examples of such curved faience rods of varying widths in the collection.

The inscription *ꜥnḫ Rꜥ-Ḥr-ꜣḫty* is finely carved. The eye and beak of the falcon are incised in detail and the cap-like head feathers end at a line dividing the neck from the wing. The overlapping upper-wing feathers are followed by the straight ones at the end which overlap the long tail feathers. Those on the belly and thighs are finely chiselled. The disk worn by the falcon and those in the *ꜣḫt* signs have the uraeus raised in the centre front. The *ꜥnḫ* hangs from the *ꜣḫt* signs, and one specifically carved stands in front of the bird. The surface of the chalky limestone has been worked to give a smooth flat facing.

53. A detailed carving of the falcon in part of the early form of the Aten name. (H. 8 cm.).

THE INTERMEDIATE FORM OF THE ATEN NAME

There are many examples of the conventional spelling of the early and late names of the Aten on inscriptions in the Collection. But there are also two examples of a transitional form in which the *Ḥr* is written phonetically. Professor Fairman pointed out the rarity of this, known only in its complete form on a mould for a faience cartouche in the Berlin Museum. The two examples in this Collection show for the first time that the second cartouche of this intermediate form is identical with that in the later form of the name.[1]

One example is in a double cartouche on the upper arm of a red quartzite figure in sunk relief. The forearm bends upwards from the elbow and is presumably a royal figure offering to or worshipping the Aten.

The spelling from right to left is:— *ʿnḫ rʿ Ḥr-3ḫty ḥʿy m 3ḫt m rn.f m itiʾ m itn.*

The second example is from an alabaster stela near the "roll" at the top. The hieroglyphs are incised and filled with blue paste or "frit". There is one complete pair of Aten cartouches with the Aten names and the remains of two more cartouches on the broken left edge of the fragment.

The spelling in the complete cartouches is from left to right:— *ʿnḫ rʿ Ḥr-3ḫty ḥʿy m 3ḫt m rn.f m itiʾ m itn.*

On the left of the fragment, the broken cartouches show the same full spelling of *Ḥr-3ḫty* but written from right to left. In the top cartouche the *ḫ* remains and *m 3ḫt*. In the lower cartouche, the *ʿnḫ rʿ 3ḫty* and the *ḫ* with part of the *r* and the *ḥ* below it.

Lit. [1]H. W. Fairman, *C/A III*, p. 183; J. Samson, *idem*, p. 231, pl. CVIII.

[UC 098]
Provenance: Amarna. Red quartzite. Height 6 cm.

[UC 351]
Provenance: Amarna. Alabaster. Height 6·5 cm.

54a. Two rare examples of the intermediate spelling of the Aten name. (H. 6·5 cm., 6 cm.).

102

54b. *Tracing of the intermediate form of the Aten name as on plate 54a. (H. 6·5 cm. and 6 cm.).*

THE COREGENCY OF AKHENATEN AND HIS SUCCESSOR

For the first time on plates 55A and 55B and 55C (Cairo), the eight signifi-cant pieces of a private stela recording evidence of the poorly documented coregency between Akhenaten and his successor are published together. Of the seven fragments found by Petrie, the four which make up the top right corner with the double cartouches of the Kings on the obverse face, were not joined when the stela was published previously.[1] The eighth piece, found in 1934, is from Cairo. It is the bottom, right corner and joins the border on the obverse side. On the reverse is a portrait of the private owner of the stela.[2]

Carved on fine limestone, the stela is in the shape of a false door. On the obverse, a small section of the torus roll and cavetto cornice remains above the raised, right border. This is carved in sunk relief with lotuses arranged in floral cones and offerings of fish. The carving is superior to that in the recessed central area. In this, at the top right corner, are two pairs of cartouches placed as in a coregency.

The first pair contain the *nomen* and *pre-nomen* of Akhenaten: *Nfr-ḫprw R'* *w'-n-R' 3ḫ-n-'Itn* ("Beautiful are the forms of Re, the unique one of Re, Akhenaten"). In the second pair are the names of his coregent: *'nḫ-ḫprw-R' mry-w'-n-R'* and *Nfr-nfrw-'Itn-mry-3ḫ-n-'Itn*, ("Living are the forms of Re, beloved of the unique one of Re, beautiful are the beauties of the Aten, beloved of Akhenaten"). So far, in two other known inscriptions recording the names of the two kings in the coregency the actual name of Akhenaten appears. In the cartouches on Tutankhamen's box, the names are associated as *'Ankhkheprure' mr (y) Neferkheprure'* ("Living are the forms of Re, beloved of Beautiful are the forms of Re") and *Nfr-nfrw-itn mry w'-n-R',*[3]

[UC 410]
Provenance: Amarna. Painted lime-stone. Length of the right-hand border in the Collection 25·0 cm. Full length with the Cairo bottom corner 41·0 cm. (Cairo, **JE 64959).** Lit. [1]J. Samson, *C/A III*, pp. 231-232, pl. CVII (2 and 3), and pl. CVIII; [2] J. D. S. Pendlebury, *idem*, p. 45 (34/42), pl. LXXIII (8 and 9); H. W. Fairman, *idem*, pp. 232-233. Comparisons: [3]P. E. Newberry, *J.E.A. XIV*, p. 4/5; [4]A. H. Gardiner, *idem*, p. 10; [5]N. de G. Davies, *RTA, passim.*

Now three examples. See p. 132.

103

104

which corresponds to the association of the names on the graffito from the Theben tomb of Pere.

See p. 131.

Left of the cartouche with Akhenaten's *pre-nomen* are the faint remains of two larger cartouches with the inscription effaced (probably those of the Aten). Left of these, in the centre, is a poorly carved disk of the Aten with descending rays. It is flanked by the remains of the stereotyped inscription: on the right, facing right; two on the left, facing left.

Under the second cartouche to the left of the raised border is a defaced column of inscription. In it are the remains of what Krauss discerned to be the name of Ankhesenpa-aten. The inscription is shallow and barely legible but he noted part of an *Ankh*, beside an *S*, above the indentations remaining from an *N*. The stone is then broken, but below the break is part of the seated figure of a female determinative and the space between it and the *N* is sufficient for *pa* and *Aten* to have been written. This suggests that the young figure on the right was probably Ankhesenpa-aten beneath her own name, following one of the two coregents named above, just as the princesses so often followed their parents as they worshipped the Aten.

The chipping away of the Aten names from the surface on the fragment on the left of the four cartouches suggests anti-Atenism. The names of the two kings had been inserted and they remain; but the presumed family scene below, of worshipping the Aten, has been smashed away.

Three other relatable fragments in the Collection are shown on the left of plate 55a. On the obverse, the largest fragment is the lower left piece of the stela. In the corner made by the left border and the bottom edge is part of the recessed central area. In this, on a platform with two raised horizontal lines, is the right leg, and part of the left, of a figure facing right, and wearing a lightly incised robe or sash which flares out in a point behind the right leg. The small fragment on its right has a sandalled foot; this piece has a very broken surface. On the third fragment, above these, is part of a robe incised on the left of the abdomen of a figure also facing right. The navel is shown. Faint traces of red paint remain on the figure in all three fragments.

The bottom right-hand corner of the stela, now in Cairo, was found by Pendlebury in 1934 and later identified as part of this stela by Professor Fairman. On the obverse face of it, the right-hand border is continued, and part of the raised base. In the recessed area of this corner is the right edge of the platform with two raised horizontal lines as in the left corner of the stela shown on plate 55a. Standing on the right edge of this platform, carved in *bas-relief*, is a figure from the waist down. It faces left, there are sandals on the feet. At first sight it appears nude, but in front of it is a line on the stone which could be a beginning of the carving of a gown. The navel is shown; the hips and thighs are plump; the body bends forward from the hips as though offering to the Aten and the knees are slightly bent in this pose. In front of this figure is an unidentifiable shape which could be the leg of another figure, behind which a line is sketched which could also be the placing of the falling edge of a gown, and below this, by the ankle, is a short horizontal line that could be to mark the end of it or a sash.

Plate 55c.

On the reverse face of the top and left edge of the stela, formed by the four joined pieces, are the head and shoulders of a kneeling portrait of the

owner, facing right. He is represented as a nobleman wearing the gold
collar. The figure is carefully carved and some of the original coloured paint
remains on the face and the wig which is bound by a fillet and crowned by
a cone of unguent (?). His thin right arm, with two bracelets on the forearm,
is lifted in acknowledgement; the hand is raised in front of his face (an
incorrectly placed *left* hand) and his other hand is in front of it. The break
in the stone is below the elbow and across the body under the shoulder.

Above the figure are traces of three vertical columns. The column on the
left edge of the stela is so badly damaged that it is not possible to see if it had
been finished or inscribed. The middle column reads: /// *Pr-n-p3-'Itn*, perhaps to be restored (*Pr-ḥ'y*)-*m-p3-'Itn*; and the inside column, of which only
the lower part is preserved, finishes with *'ir ʿ*, perhaps for the title *'iry-ʿ3*
"doorkeeper", although an unusual writing of it. On one of the three small
fragments, the hieroglyphs for *pr-mrt-n* remain, with *t3 dỉ* (?) and *ʿ* (*ayin*) in
the next column.

On the reverse of the Cairo piece, of the bottom left corner of the stela, is
the lower part of the kneeling body of the owner. The pleats of his robe are
shown passing diagonally behind his body, and around his hips is the pleated
and fully flared kilt of the courtier. The chest and the body are finely carved
but the foot on which the body rests is stylised. The toes rest on the top of
the lower edge of the stela. In front of his knees are unexplained pleats
hanging vertically.

PART II

I   PREFACE

When the first edition of this book was written the aim was to introduce some of the key pieces from Amarna in the Petrie Collection at University College, London. The emphasis was on fragments which show the quality attained in the arts and crafts in this city of the mid-fourteenth century B.C. Objects of historical significance were included which, as then described, span the whole period down to the stela with the unique evidence of Akhenaten and his coregent.

In 1973 a new direction and additional impetus was given to research on the period by Professor John R. Harris who in two articles published his view that "Nefernefruaten Nefertiti" and "Smenkhkare" were the same person, i.e., that Nefertiti succeeded Akhenaten as Pharaoh. These, and further articles by him are discussed in Part II of this, the second edition. More key pieces from the Petrie Collection are included: and the resulting evidence of research on them and on other material from and at Amarna, supports his conclusions.

Available information about the last years at Amarna is reviewed, with evidence of Nefertiti's "power" and "importance" in the earliest years of Akhenaten's reign at Thebes, now being pieced together by Dr. Redford and his team on the building blocks (*talatat*) of the Akhenaten Temple.

Julia Samson 1978

Fig. 1

Fig. 2

Fig. 3

Fig. 4

Fig. 5

Fig. 6

II SUMMARY OF DEVELOPMENTS IN ROYAL NAMES AND TITLES

In Thebes the Queen's short name was Nefertiti with a queenly figure as her image (Fig. 1).

There, the King Amenhotep IV changed his name to Akhenaten to include the god Aten; and Nefertiti's was changed to Nefernefru-aten-Nefertiti, to include the Aten. In this, the Queen's long name, the god's name is written backwards so that it faces the Queen's image, which was a phenomenal honour (Fig. 2).

At Amarna Nefertiti's short name was almost entirely superseded by her long name which, with her titles Great Wife of the King, Beloved of him, is ubiquitous in inscriptions. (p. 111)

At Amarna Nefertiti's long name was duplicated in adjacent cartouches resembling a king's prenomen (first name) and nomen (throne name). (Fig. 3). This practice was followed by Queen Tawosret who, in the Nineteenth Dynasty, doubled her own name before assuming kingly titles.

Late in Akhenaten's reign at Amarna Nefertiti changed her wifely title *ḥmt nsw wrt* (which Meritaten adopted) to *ḥmt nsw 'ȝt,* (Fig. 4) with little difference in meaning. (Queen Hatshepsut and Queen Ta-wosret who both ruled as kings, eventually abandoned their wifely titles) (p. 126).

Akhenaten's coregent (inscriptions show their joint rule) (Fig. 5) was named Nefernefruaten (Nefertiti's Aten name), with her own title Beloved of Akhenaten, and a new prenomen Ankhkheprure, - Beloved of Akhenaten. This was sometimes spelt with a *.t* to show it was feminine (Fig. 6). (The pattern of these names is parallel to that used by the three queens known to have ruled as kings, who kept their queenly names and an epithet and added a new prenomen) (p. 131).

Akhenaten and Nefertiti's eldest daughter Meritaten and at least one of her sisters, when they were young children, were called not only "King's Daughter" but also "King's Wife" which points to the last title being an honorific for princesses (p.128-9). Meritaten is described later as "King's Great Wife", as Sitamen was in the previous reign in relation to her father Amenhotep III. Meritaten is thus described in an inscription where she is shown with both her father, to whom this title possibly related, and his coregent King Ankhkheprure-Nefernefruaten. This differentiates Meritaten from Akhenaten's successor. (Fig. 7).

The prenomen Ankhkheprure has been found used with the epithet *mry-ỉtn,* "Beloved of the Aten." In one instance they are in the same cartouche. This is paired with another cartouche containing the name Nefernefruaten, with the name of the Aten partly reversed to face a kingly figure with a "king's beard", a flail and a kingly sceptre (Fig. 8). (Queen Hatshepsut as ruler is portrayed with the traditional attachment of a "king's beard" with the other regalia (p. 127).

The prenomen of Akhenaten's coregent was retained with the new throne name Smenkhkare-djeserkhepru (Fig. 9). This throne name has not been found combined with the name Nefernefruaten which it possibly replaced; nor with the epithet "Beloved of Akhenaten", as though it were used after Akhenaten's death. (p. 113).

I am very grateful to Dr. Geoffrey Martin for sparing precious time to draw the inscriptions in Part II of this book, except for Figure 5 for which I am greatly indebted to Professor H. S. Smith.

Fig. 7

Fig. 8   Fig. 9

1. Ägyptisches Museum 21972.
2. Wilson *JNES* 32 (1973) p. 238

III   MORE KEY PIECES

1.   NEFERTITI'S NAMES AND TITLES

The changes in Nefertiti's names and titles have recently been under close scrutiny. They are an indication of her importance in the historical developments of the Amarna period; and are inextricably part of the history of Akhenaten's reign and that of his successor.

(i)   In Thebes. The first change occurred in Thebes where, just as the King's name was changed from Amenophis (IV) to Akhenaten to include the Aten, so Nefertiti's was lengthened to Nefernefruaten-Nefertiti to include the Aten. On the scarab plate 51a, Nefertiti's name can be presumed to have been behind the King's, on the left edge now broken away. If her cartouche matched the King's it probably contained her short name, contemporary with his earlier one. In West Berlin there is a fragment of blue faience with the King's early name Amenhotep beside the Queen's early name Nefertiti.[1] It seems likely that the changes in the two names would have occurred simultaneously or very close in time. Wilson saw the addition of a new name by Nefertiti as "a dogmatic assertion of a religious nature similar to the doctrinal proclamation made by a king when he assumed his prenomen at Accession."[2] Its effect at the time could have been to show the Queen's affinity with the King.

(ii)   Nefertiti's short name; Plate 56. There are two examples of the Queen's short name in the Collection as shown on plate 56. The alabaster (calcite) carving evidently came from a large inscription; the other is on a small fragment of white faience with the lower part of the Queen's name and her image inlaid in purple; part of another cartouche is similarly inlaid beside it, presumably from Akhenaten's name. The stone fragment was not published by Petrie but can be accepted as part of his finds. The smaller faience piece he published in *Scarabs.*[1] He recorded in *Tell el Amarna*[2] another example of the Queen's short name on a stela from the central palace, which was one of the early buildings containing the earlier Amarna art forms as well as the later styles for which see plates 20 and 27.

1. Petrie, *Scarabs* XXXVI; 18.10.44 (not shown).
2. P. *T/A* pl. XII(2)

(iii)   The date of the change in Nefertiti's name at Amarna. There is an indication of the early date of the few occurrences of Nefertiti's short name at Amarna on Boundary Stela K.[1] Although her short

1. Lepsius *Denkmäler* Abb. III, bl. 110(b)

56. *Nefertiti's short name. Fragment of inlaid faience (H.3cm., W.2 cm). Part of alabaster calcite inscription (H.11.5 cm. W.12.5 cm.).*

Plate 56
UC 22994 and 12469
Provenance Amarna, stone inscription. H.11.5 cm W.12.5 cm. Unpublished. Faience fragment H.3 cm. W.2 cm. Petrie *Scarabs* Pl. *XXXVI.* 18.10.44

57. *Nefertiti's long name: a.(H.8.5 cm., W.7.5 cm.); b. & c. doubled; d. & e. Akhenaten's two names; f. & g. The Aten's two names.*

a

UC 2261
Plate 57 a.
Provenance; the royal residence Amarna. H.8.5 cm. W.7.5 cm.
b. UC 23098b. c. UC 1919. d. UC 2383E. e. UC 1914. f. UC 1902. g. UC 1905. Provenance Amarna. Moulds, red clay; Average H.3.2 cm W.3 cm. Faience plaques faded pale green; average unbroken examples H.2 cm. W.1.5 cm.

b

c

d

e

f

g

name appears in the body of the text, her long name was added behind her on the extreme right edge of the stela where her second daughter Maketaten has been "crudely inserted".[2] The change seems, therefore, to have occurred during the carving of this stela (which is one of those with the early form of the dedication of the site) and around the time of the birth of Maketaten. This is discussed on p. 125.

2. Davies *RTA* V p. 25

(iv) Nefertiti's long name; Plate 57. In the Queen's long name the writing of the god's name Aten is reversed so that it faces the determinative of the queenly image in her original name Nefertiti.[1] This phenomenon stresses her link with the god in the most certain terms and in a startlingly noticeable way for all to see in the multitudinous inscriptions. The spelling of the name varies slightly, but the form at a, Plate 57 is from the painted mural that Petrie removed from the royal residence opposite the central palace. It comes from a scene, the lower part of which is in the Ashmolean Museum, Oxford,[2] of the royal children grouped round their parents.[3] Painted by court artists and seen constantly by the King and Queen it can be accepted as the normal form. Wilson wrote "the reversed writing in a cartouche is so unusual that it stands out in the texts with an emphasis like capitalized letters in modern writing."[4] The occasions when the Aten is not reversed to face the Queen's image are so extremely rare that they can be looked upon as exceptions which prove the rule. In all the inscriptions recorded by Davies in *The Rock Tombs of El Amarna,*[5] the writer has found only one example where the Aten does not face the Queen's image, and that is an exception in that tomb.[6]

1. S. Tawfik, *MDIK* 29.1 (1973) pp. 82-86

2. Ashmolean Museum No. 1893.1.4. (267).
3. Nina de Garis Davies; *JEA* 17 (1921) pl. 2.

4. Wilson *op. cit.* p. 238.

5. Davies. *The Rock Tombs of EL AMARNA.* I–VI. (1903–1908).
6. Davies, *RTA,* III, pl. XXVII.

The Queen's long name is found ubiquitously throughout inscriptions large and small, at and from Amarna, with the titles Great Wife of the King and "Beloved" of the King.

(v) The doubled cartouches; Plate 57. Evidence of change in the presentation of Nefertiti's long name lies in the red clay moulds and the faience impressions made in them showing two adjacent cartouches both containing her long name.[1] The mould (plate 57b) and part of a glazed cartouche-plaque (c) resemble in form the adjacent cartouches with the two names of the King (d and e) and the two names of the Aten (f and g). Of the Aten names, in this unusual form of a god's name in a cartouche, the twelve examples in the Collection are the earlier form i.e., before c. year 9.

As Harris has written, Nefertiti's status of kingship "may be further confirmed by the otherwise unexplained duplication of her cartouche as though, like a king, she possessed a prenomen and nomen."[2] The device is strikingly paralleled by the action of Queen Tawosret in the nineteenth dynasty.[3] She doubled her name,[4] possibly before adopting the full titles of a reigning monarch at the death of her husband when she apparently discarded the wifely title *ḥmt nsw (wrt).*[5]

1. J. Samson, *CdE* XLVIII.96 (1973) p.247 Fig. 2. and *CdE* L.101 (1976) pp 34-5; Fig. 2.
2. J. Harris, *Acta Or.* XXXV(1973) p.13.
3. J. Harris *Acta Or.* 36 (1974) N.51.
4. Vernier, *Bijoux et Orfevreries CCG.* (1907) p. 97 Nos. 52264-65.
5. Hayes *Scepter of Egypt* (1968) p. 357.

The arrangement of Nefertiti's name varies slightly within the doubled cartouches as it does when written singly. Confusion possibly arose from writing the same name to read from opposite sides while at the same time reversing the writing of the Aten to face the determinative of the Queen's image.

Petrie records thirty-two moulds with the Queen's name doubled of which eighteen are in the Collection, as well as one green faience plaque (broken) from such a mould.[6] In these moulds, the writing in the left cartouche reads from left to right, and conversely in the right cartouche in which the writing of the Aten is reversed to face the Queen's image.[7] Three similar moulds in the British Museum show the same arrangement of the writing; and of the two blue faience plaques there, at least one was made in such a mould and probably the other although this is not so clearly legible. These were incorrectly drawn in the *Catalogue of Egyptian Scarabs in the British Museum* where the Aten is not shown facing the Queen's image in the one cartouche.[8] The significance of this unprecedented iconography in the Queen's name was presumably unexpected in 1913, and was missed.

6. P.*T/A* pl. XV(82); the plaque which Petrie records is impressed from a *typical mould.*
7. J. Samson *CdE* XLVIII 96(1973) Fig. 2.
8. Hall, *Cat. of Egyptian Scarabs in the BM.* Vol.1. (1913) Nos. 1966, BM 21937; 1977, BM 40897; Moulds BM Nos. 24953; 26840; 26841. The incorrect Museum drawing was copied in *CdE* L.101(1976) Fig.2,3/4 by the present author, who thanks Mrs Blankenberg of The Hague for drawing attention to the original mistake.

58. *Names of Akhenaten's successor: a. & b. Prenomen with feminine .t ; i. with nomen Smenkhkare (H.1.5 cm., W.1.7 cm.). See also Fig. 5 and plate 55c.*

Plate 58.
f. UC 12491. g. UC 1923.
a. UC 12487. b. UC 12485. c. UC 1924. d. UC 23774. e. UC 12484. Provenance Amarna Moulds red clay Average H.3 to 4 cm. W.3 cm. Ring bezels blue faience, average H.2 cm to 1.5 cm. W.1 cm. to .5 cm.

2. THE NAMES OF AKHENATEN'S COREGENT AND SUCCESSOR; Plate 58

The prenomen of Akhenaten's coregent and successor was Ankhkheprure. There are faience ring bezels in the Collection with this name alone (f); and clay moulds in which they were made; an impression from a mould is at (g).[1]

There are also examples of this prenomen with the epithet "Beloved of Akhenaten" (a-e). In this phrase usually the King's prenomen is written, (b and e); or his epithet (a, c and d).

1. P.*T/A* pl. XV (92-102). 2P. *idem* (92-96); 3.P. *idem* (93/94). See also *Scarabs* pl. XXXVII (1-8).

Petrie recorded twenty-six examples of the names of the King linked with the prenomen of his successor in the one cartouche;[2] in eight instances the latter is spelt with a .t which makes the prenomen of the coregent and successor a feminine name.[3] Two examples with the .t are in the Collection (a and b) and are drawn below (examples in other collections are noted (p. 114).

2P. idem (92-96);

3.P. idem (93/94). See also Scarabs pl. XXXVII (1-8).

On the coregency stela (plate 55a) one of Akhenaten's two cartouches has his prenomen and epithet Neferkhkheprure Waenre, and the other his nomen Akhenaten. The other two cartouches have the prenomen of King Ankhkheprure, and epithet Beloved of Waenre, and the nomen Nefernefruaten (Nefertiti's Aten name), Beloved of Akhenaten (her epithet).

The nomen Smenkhkare does not appear on this stela.

The development of the coregent and successor's names based on available evidence appears to be as follows:-

a) the prenomen Ankhkheprure was used throughout; sometimes with a .t; making it feminine; sometimes alone.

b) mostly the prenomen was linked with Akhenaten as "Beloved" by him; and when used in conjunction with the nomen Nefernefruaten, this too was linked with Akhenaten as "Beloved" by him. The names thus linked with Akhenaten must be presumed to have been used in his life-time.

c) The nomen Smenkhkare has not been found in conjunction with the nomen Nefernefruaten, as though it replaced the latter;

d) the nomen Smenkhkare has not been found linked with Akhenaten, as though it were used after his death (p. 132).

On plate 58 is a ring bezel (h) with the successor's nomen and epithet, Smenkhkare-djeserkhepru.[4] On the broken clay seal (i) are two cartouches; the prenomen Ankhkheprure in the one on the left; and the nomen Smenkhkare in the one on the right, with djeser, part of the epithet, below it. Above the cartouches is the sky sign pt and on the right of the seal is part of an oval curve which apparently encircled the inscription.[5] It resembles a clay seal with an enveloping oval found by Pendlebury in the north suburb.[6] On this the cartouches are surmounted by nswt bity and below them is t3/wy/:(nb, is missing). (See Fig. 9)

Plate 58.
h. UC 23801. H.2 cm. W.1 cm.
i. UC 12492 H.1.5 cm. W.1.7 cm.
Provenance Amarna; Decayed blue faience bezel; black clay seal.
4. P.T/A pl. XV 103-105; Scarabs pl. XXXVII; 18.11.9.
5. J. Samson CdE XLVIII, 96 (1973) Fig. 1. p. 244.
6. Pendlebury C/A 11 pl. L.29/341 pp. 25-29/275; see also p. 27 (29/29 (sic))

(i). The Feminine Name (Figs. 10 and 11).

The addition of a .t to the prenomen of Akhenaten's coregent, which prenomen was retained by his successor, can only be regarded as a means of making the name feminine. There is no satisfactory grammatical or other reason for the .t except to make a masculine name, or one of ambiguous gender, unmistakably feminine. Petrie published the two types of ring bezels that he found with a .t in the name and/or epithet of the coregent. But he missed the significance of the fact that it makes the name of Akhenaten's successor a feminine one. In his transliterations the .t remains unrecorded;[1] and it remained so, as such, until 1973.[2]

Plate 58.
a and b, as described above, and drawn below.

Of the twenty six names of the coregent written with the prenomen and epithet "Beloved of Neferkheprure" or "Beloved of Waenre" which Petrie recorded in Tell el Amarna (1894), as noted above,

1. P. Scarabs (1917) p. XXXVII; 18.11. P. T/A (1894) pl. XV.93-94.
2. J. Samson CdE XLVIII, 96 (1973) pp. 243-244.

3. P. *Kahun, Gurob and Hawara* (1890)
pl. XXIII (21) and P. *Scarabs* (1917)
pl. XXXVII. 18.11. (2–5).
4. J. Samson *CdE* XLVIII.96(1973)
Fig. 1.

Fig. 10   Fig. 11

5. R. Krauss. *Hildesheimer Ägyptologische Beitrage*, 7, 1978,   Das
Ende der Amarnazeit; Preussischer
Kulturbesitz 21941; Ägyptisches Museum 25108.
6. Hall *Cat. Egyptian Scarabs in the
BM* (1913) No. 2869 BM 50953.

7. MMA 10.136.935.

8. J. Harris *CdE* XLVIII.96(1973)
Postscript p. 250. a) Carter obj. no.
48h; McLeod, *Composite Bows from
the Tomb of Tutankhamun* pl. XVII
inscr.4.2: (b) Carter obj. no. 481(2);
McLeod *op. cit.* Pl.XVII inscr.6.2.

eight were written with the recognisable *.t.* Another was recorded in *Kahun, Gurob and Hawara* (1890)[3] before he excavated at Amarna. Later, in 1917, he included some in his book *Scarabs and Cylinders with Names*[4] but the numbers do not correspond with those in *Tell el Amarna,* so it is not possible to know how many were extant in his day.

Instances of the successor's prenomen and/or epithet spelt with a *.t* are now being traced in museums, either unrecorded or wrongly registered. This illumines one reason for the past lack of recognition of the evidence from Amarna that Akhenaten's coregent and success- or was a woman. Now the signpost is recognised more examples may well be found.

Of the eight instances in *Tell el Amarna* which Petrie found with a *.t,* one of each of the two types is in the Collection (as at Figures 10 and 11).[4] On plate 58 the ring bezel (a) reads *ʿnḫ.t-ḫprw-Rʿ mr.t wʿ-n-Rʿ*; and the one (b) *ʿnḫ-ḫprw-Rʿ mr.t nfr-ḫprw-Rʿ.*

Two examples of the *.t* in both the name and epithet (a) are on moulds in Berlin.[5] They are from the German excavations over a decade after Petrie's. The fact that they are moulds suggests a recog- nised formula for mass reproduction.

One blue ring bezel reading the same as (a) (and Figure 10) is in the British Museum. This was recorded and reproduced by Hall[6] in 1913 as "Ankh-kheperu-Maat-en-Ra Ua-en-Ra (Smenkhara)." It is now known from inscriptions large and small that the coregent's epithet was *mry(t)* "Beloved" of Akhenaten; Maat in this context makes no sense. But without our recognition of the *.t* as a feminine ending, Hall was misled, because at one end of the pool sign (*mry*) the tiny upright is blurred and this, with the additional *.t* in what was viewed as a man's name, he read as Maat. This reading ignores the *.t* under the Ankh which Hall reproduced as a thin stroke.

In the Metropolitan Museum, New York, there is a bezel of the same type as (b) (and Figure 11) which was a gift in 1910; its proven- ance is unknown.[7]

Harris has recorded from the tomb of Tutankhamen the use of the feminine form of *mrt.f* which "related originally to Ankhkheprure *mry* X; and Nefernefruaten *mry* Y".[8] "On one of Tutankhamen's bows" . . . "where the cartouches are secondary usurpations, the feminine *mrt.f* stands unaltered."[a] On another bow it occurs where there is no indication of any replacement of names.[b]

(ii) *The link of Nefertiti's Aten name with the successor.* The apparent replacement of Nefertiti's Aten name Nefernefruaten by the name Smenkhkare, while retaining the prenomen Ankhkheprure, reflects events in the last years at Amarna. This is discussed more fully on p. 132 ff.

Besides being the Queen's Aten name, Nefernefruaten was the name of the fourth daughter of Akhenaten and Nefertiti and, at the death of Akhenaten, its retention as a throne name by the successor as sole king would have been inappropriate. This would be a good reason for adopting a new throne name. The fact that Nefernefruaten was the name of the Queen (and her daughter) makes the suggestion that it was used contemporaneously for another regal person, a youth as coregent (as yet unidentifiable), seem very unlikely.

In the writer's opinion this supports Harris's more recent view that, rather than two kingly persons of similar name succeeding each other with no perceptible interval, as he wrote, Nefertiti *was* the coregent, using her own Aten name and her usual epithet "Beloved of the King" whom she finally succeeded as Pharaoh, with the throne name Smenkhkare-djeserkhepru.[1]

1. J. Harris *GM* 4.(1973) pp.15-17; *Acta Or.* XXXV(1973) pp.5-14 and 36 (1974) pp. 11-21.

3. CROWNS; Plate 59

Plate 59.
a UC 24271. b UC 24272. c UC 24274. Provenance Amarna Faience.

The evidence from Amarna of what crowns were worn there and who wore them has proved of extreme historical importance in the interpretation of Amarna scenes. The age is an exceptional one; Akhenaten and Nefertiti wore similar gowns and regalia and some of the interpretations in the past have been based on wrong premises, such as the one that if an un-named figure wore a crown it must be a man, whereas it is now fully recognised that Nefertiti wore kings' crowns.

From faience examples and fragments in the Collection[1] it can be seen that Nefertiti's own distinctive flat-topped, straight-sided crown with uraeus was blue, and in these examples, (as well as on one known stone example)[2], it was covered in discs like the *Khepresh* crown. The examples in the Collection are from her inlaid portraits and from her statues.

1. J. Samson *JEA* 59 (1973) pp 47-59.
2. Cairo No. 54546, Englebach *ASAE* (1938) pl. 17. Nos. 67.21A and 43580.

(i)   Crown from an inlay

At (a) on plate 59 Nefertiti's crown from an inlay is in nearly perfect condition. It was planned and made with care and precision, glazed front and back and the high quality of the workmanship suggests it is from a portrait in a scene of delicacy and distinction, perhaps in the palace or some other significant position. It is covered with discs.

(a) UC 24271. H.3.5 cm. W.4. cm.
(b) UC 24272. Top. W.7. cm.

The straight front edge from above the forehead is glazed and unbroken. It meets the corner of the horizontal brow-line, which is unbroken to the flap (in front of the ear) now partly chipped away; - the back corner is obliquely chipped off.

The top line of the crown is unbroken and smoothly glazed. It is 5 cm. deep in the centre but thins to 0.5 cm. at the sides forming a curved inlay planned to project above the surface.

The fine glaze on the flat back of the piece is discontinued at the top left corner which is smoothly recessed as though to notch it securely into place. The top half of the back line of the crown is chipped but below that the edge is smoothly glazed. The glaze is a matt grey-blue overall, and the discs on the front of the inlay are made by two concentric circles with a hollow in the centre.

(ii)   Top of Nefertiti's crown from a statue

What remains of the glazed surface on the fragment of Nefertiti's crown from a statue, (b), is part of the flat top, and part of a side at right angles. It is covered with discs. All the edges of the fragment are broken. The core is rough and chalky with a sketchily made

UC 24272
Plate 59(b)
Dark blue matt glaze; patchy colour. H. of glazed side 2 cm. W. glazed top 7 cm.

a

b

c

d

cavity near the centre, presumably for the head of the statue. The glaze on the outside of the crown is a matt dark blue which is unevenly faded with deep blue remaining on top but patches of reddened colour in the glaze. The discs have an outside ring and an inside circular recess.

The piece is placed (out of scale) on the sketch (d).

(iii) Part of base and back streamer of Nefertiti's crown.

The two fragments joined vertically down the centre on plate 59 (c) are the curved base of the back of the Queen's crown, with the end of the tie from the decorated encircling band as on the Berlin limestone head, which is sketched (d). The pattern of the tie was probably imprinted in the glaze from the mould in which the back of the crown was made.

The fragment is from a statue; the bottom rim is 2 cm. deep and inside it sloped gradually upwards as it turns to what must have been a concave centre. The interior is unglazed but scored horizontally which would help to secure it on the head of a statue. All the edges of the piece are broken except the bottom rim. The glazed surface, which is covered with discs, is now matt and a faded blue, but in

116

small patches, particularly round the edge of the bottom rim, there are traces of the deeper blue.

Unlike the flat painted pattern of the streamer at the back of the crown on the famous painted portrait-head in Berlin, the faience pattern is recessed as though for small inlays or to give emphasis by light and dark alternatives. The drop petals which are hollowed at the bottom of the tie are surmounted by four squares which continue up the side (simplified to stripes on the painted crown). In the centre the cross-bars divide recessed rectangles.

There are in the Collection, other blue faience crowns and fragments of crowns, covered with discs. Two small Khepresh crowns from inlaid scenes are in the bottom left corner of plate VI. The *curved* fragments are obviously from statues of either Akhenaten or Nefertiti, some apparently of life-size. For these the crowns were probably made in moulds in two halves, just as the large faience bunches of grapes were from Amarna*. One small mould for an inlaid crown in the top left corner of plate 50, has the raised circles which produce the incised discs on the faience examples.

* UC 1700

From a study of the *faience* fragments of wigs and crowns from Amarna statues and inlays in the Petrie Collection, it certainly appears that all these head-dresses were blue. The colour and condition of the glaze now ranges from those pieces with the bright "royal" blue often with a high gloss remaining, to many with a matt surface and the colour reduced to pale blue, green-blue, grey-blue, green and grey, some with patches of red from the composition of the glaze. The very small Khepresh crown on the bottom left of plate VI, is made of lapis-lazuli coloured blue glass, now only discernible through a tiny chip in the lilac-grey patina which covers the crown. But where the faience fragments of head-dresses from Amarna have faded or changed colour, patches of the deep blue often remain on sheltered rims or where the glaze has run over onto protected inner surfaces.

In stone reliefs and statues, neither Nefertiti's blue crown nor the *Khepresh* crown is usually shown with the discs carved, possibly because of the time such repetition would take on stone. There is one stone relief of Akhenaten wearing the Khepresh crown covered with discs in the Royal Scottish Museum, Edinburgh; this is described as a model.[1] Nefertiti's distinctive crown on a limestone statue-head in Cairo is decorated with discs;[2] as is Akhenaten's *Khepresh*-crown on a stone statue-head there;[3] and Tutankhamen's *Khepresh* crown on his stone statue from the coronation group in New York, in this particularly symbolic setting of his kingship.[4] But in malleable gold there are numerous examples of the Khepresh crown worn by him which are covered in discs, both in statues and reliefs from his tomb; and in gold relief Ankhesenamen's cap-crowns are also thus decorated.[5] Gold, like faience can be impressed. No gold or faience examples of Nefertiti's cap-crown are known to the writer but so many of the Amarna patterns were carried over into the next reign that it is not unlikely Nefertiti's cap-crown also had discs on it. They are not shown on the *painted* cap-crown she wears on her standing statue in Berlin;[6] but then neither are they painted on her

1. C. Aldred, *Akhenaten and Nefertiti* (1973) pl. 12.
2. Cairo 34546, Englebach, *ASAE* XXXVIII (1938) pp 95-107; pl. XVII.
3. Englebach *idem.*
4. Hayes, *Scepter of Egypt* (1968) Fig. 186. MMA

5. I. Edwards *Treasures of Tutankhamen* 22; and the golden Shrine 25;
6. Ägyptisches Museum; Berlin; Reg. No. 21263.

distinctive crown on the well known Berlin limestone statue-head (Plate 4).

4. KIYA; Plate 60

There is in the Collection a narrow strip of carved wood with a rounded hole at the top end; if a wooden dowel were fitted into this hole it could act as a hinge and the strip could be swung aside. It resembles the lid of a pen box. Its interest lies in the remains of an inscription in a column down the centre of the strip: this includes the name of Kiya. It was first published by Harris in 1974 in an article in which he collected, for comparison, the rare and neglected instances of the name Kiya, and the following is largely based on his findings.[1]

On the lid the letter .t remains to the right of and above a cartouche containing the prenomen and epithet of Akhenaten. Below this is the name Kiya written in the usual way. (Fig. 12).

The full and apparently standard inscription usual with Kiya's name includes the title "King's Wife" (Fig. 13). This brings Kiya, the owner of the box(?) into the Amarna royal circle as a royal wife or consort of Akhenaten, but not as *Great* Royal Wife and her name is not in a cartouche. The name with the accompanying formula has been found on a cosmetic vessel in the Metropolitan Museum, New York;[2] on the coffin used in Tomb 55 in the Valley of the Kings[3] about the occupant of which so much controversy has arisen, and on a block from Hermopolis.[4] Harris notes the uniformity of the text surrounding the name which has facilitated his detection of palimpsests where these occur. One particular example of this is on a block from Hermopolis where an inscription stands in relation to the portrait of a lady wearing a particular wig. The portrait was apparently originally designed to represent Kiya, part of whose usual accompanying text is still visible. But the inscription in the adjacent column relates to a daughter of the King, thought to be Meritaten.[5] This bears out Harris's important findings in a total review of such palimpsest fragments in inscriptions from Maru Aten as well as Hermopolis, of which he writes: "in every case where the original text is discernible it is suggestive of Kiya. Conversely there is no positive evidence for the erasure or alteration of any inscription of Nefertiti - and this applies also to other instances of her alleged deletion in favour of Meritaten. In short", he writes, "it would seem to be Kiya whose name was replaced at Maru-Aten and elsewhere, nor is there anything left to substantiate the 'disgrace' and demotion of Nefertiti."[6] This could relegate the damage to her name or features, where it does occur, largely to the not unusual destruction in ancient Egypt of royal figures by subsequent builders.

Kiya remains a shadowy figure so far, a secondary wife or concubine of Akhenaten. Her name occurs with the earlier and later forms of the Aten and she was still favoured in year 11. This, Harris notes, would have enabled her to have been the mother of Tutankhaten and not improbably of the two youngest princesses Meritaten-the-younger and Ankhesenpa-aten-the-younger.[7] He suggests that injuries to her

Plate 60
UC 24382
L.9.7 cm. W.3.7 cm. Provenance Amarna; Wood

1. J. Harris *CdE* XLIX;97(1974) pp. 25-30.

Fig. 12   Fig. 13

2. Hayes *Scepter of Egypt 2*; (1968) p. 294.
3. H. Fairman *JEA* XLVII (1961) p. 29.
4. Roeder *Amarna Reliefs aus Hermopolis* pls. 32; 57; (153. VIII).
5. J. Cooney, *Amarna Reliefs from Hermopolis* (1965) p. 34 (no. 18.b), J. Harris, *op. cit.* p. 27: n.4 gives 12 examples of traces of Kiya's formula beneath a secondary formula.

6. J. Harris *op. cit.* pp. 25-30.
7. Harris *op. cit.* N. 6.

portrait and erasures of her name may have meant her death or decline in importance, and he warns against the risk of repeating the mistake made over Nefertiti, by suggesting she "fell from grace". (See also page 130).

IV PAST THEORIES AND LATER INFORMATION

For over a century theories have been promulgated about the physical characteristics of Akhenaten. His body has not been found, and the theories are mostly based on the exaggerated carvings customary in the art near the beginning of his reign, which can now be seen to have been moderated as the years passed. Some of these theories have blocked the way to a fuller understanding of the period and it is necessary today to re-assess them when considering the newer information given in detail in the next section. Those mentioned here, very briefly, show some of the problems which have arisen. They began in the middle of the last century.

In 1855 Mariette suggested that Akhenaten was a eunuch.[1] In 1891 Lefébure opined that Akhenaten was a woman.[2] In 1894 Petrie's record of his excavations at Amarna appeared in which he asks: "Is it credible that the most uxorious king of Egypt, who appears with his wife on every monument, who rides side by side with her in her chariot, and kisses her in public (tomb of Mahu), who dances her on his knee, who has a steadily increasing family - that this king was either a woman in masquerade or an eunuch? Further, see the essential differences shewn anatomically between the figures of the king and his wife; however much good living and luxurious habits may have plumped his figure, it is distinctly that of a man, in contrast to his wife beside him."[3]

A wealth of material remains at and from Amarna, but ideas have continued to be advanced in this century which appear to rest on inferences that the material cannot substantiate. These include the assumption that indications show Akhenaten had a complaint known as "Fröhlich's Syndrome" which, based on his portraits in the early art-form that was later modified, can never be established.[4] It has also been suggested that he probably had an unusual platycephalic skull, although Amarna royalty is not shown bareheaded except for the six princesses when young children. Of them it has been asked whether the shape of their sculptured heads did not show that they, or the pattern after which they were modelled, did not suffer from a form of hydrocephalus;[5] (see p. 15). But all six siblings would not suffer from the same disability and as adults their heads are shown as normal. Later it was recognised that the sculptured form of their heads was probably "greatly exaggerated";[6] and partly due to hairdressing.[7]

Crowns, and who wore them, as noted in the section on them above, are archaeologically important at Amarna. Nefertiti wore king's crowns on occasions. But the crown by which she is best known is the unique shape she adopted, which is worn by nobody else except Akhenaten.[8] It is on her famous limestone portrait in

60. *Wooden fragment with name of Kiya, a consort of Akhenaten whose prenomen is in the cartouche above her name (L. 9.7 cm., W. 3.7 cm.).*

1. Mariette *Bull. Arch. de L'Athenaeum français* (1855) No. 6; 57.
    2. Lefébure, *PSBA* (1891) No. 13; 479 ff. 3. P.T/A (1894) p. 39.
4. C. Aldred *Akhenaten* (1968) p.134.
5. C. Aldred *op. cit.* p. 135.
6. C. Aldred *Akhenaten and Nefertiti* (1973) No. 88.
7. J. Samson *JEA* 61 (1975) p. 263.
8. C. Aldred, *Akhenaten and Nefertiti* (1973) Fig. 31.

9. F. Giles *Ikhnaton* (1970) pl. 111.
10. Gunn, *C/A* 1 (1923) p. 155.

11. J. Harris, *CdE* (1974) XLIX; 97; pp. 25-30).
12. R. Redford *ATP.* 1. (1976) p.94.
13. Harris, *GM* 4 (1973) p. 16.
14. J. Samson, *CdE* (1973) XLVIII; 96;

15. Newberry, *JEA* 51, 1928.p.7. See C. Aldred, *Akhenaten* (1968) p. 139.
16. J. Harris, *Acta Or.* XXXV; (1973) pp. 5-13. pl. 1.

1. J. Harris *G.M.* 4(1973) pp. 15-17. *Acta Or.* XXXV (1973) pp. 5-13.
2. Schäfer; *Amtliche Berichte* 34 (1912-13), pp. 136-7. *ZÄS* 52(1915).
3. Borchardt, *Porträts der Königin Nofret-ete* (1923).
4. Newberry *JEA* 14 (1928) p. 7.

Berlin page 21(4). Nevertheless, comparatively recently, and without any evidence, this portrait has been captioned "more probably that of Ankhesenamen or Meritaten", although nowhere have the princesses been found wearing Nefertiti's distinctive crown.[9]

Arising from the re-use of the cartouches of a queen on some Amarna buildings, suggestions were made in 1923 that Nefertiti may have died or fallen into disgrace before the end of Akhenaten's reign.[10] These concepts have continued. But, as explained on p. 118, the erasures concerned have now been identified by Harris to be, not of Nefertiti's name, but of the name of Kiya, consort of Akhenaten; for use by Meritaten.[11] Evidence being uncovered at Karnak by Redford and considered by him with some Amarna inscriptions, has led him to suggest that Nefertiti possibly lived until the third year of Tutankhamen's reign.[12]

Petrie's hypothesis from his original excavation at Amarna, that Akhenaten was succeeded by a youth Ankhkheprure Smenkhkare, has been acceptable to most scholars without subsequent confirmation - until this decade. But Harris has now pointed out that there are "no positive indications that 'he' was a male."[13] In addition, the .t in the successor's name, now noted and published as such, makes it a feminine name.[14]

On the Pase Stela, found by the Germans (Berlin 17813), the two un-named figures shown on it in affectionate dalliance were originally recognised as Akhenaten and Nefertiti. This stela is fully dealt with below, but it is perhaps relevant to mention it in this section as an instance of unsubstantiated identification. Newberry published a reassessment of the royal figures, by Carter, who maintained that they were two kings because they both wore crowns. In relation to their affectionate pose, and noting the fact that the youth as co-regent bore Nefertiti's Aten name and her epithet, Newberry cited the relationship between the Emperor Hadrian and the youth Antinous; since then a number of writers have postulated a homosexual relationship between Akhenaten and the youth.[15] But Harris has pointed out that the three empty cartouches on the stela are those for a King and Queen, and do not signify a coregency.[16]

V   NEW DIRECTION AND IMPETUS GIVEN TO RESEARCH

In 1973 Harris published his short article "Nefernefruaten" followed in the same year by the longer one "Nefertiti Rediviva."[1] He had examined the details of the Pase stela which was found by the Germans excavating at Amarna. Schäfer published it in 1912-13 and recognised the two crowned, enthroned but un-named figures on it as Akhenaten and Nefertiti.[2] Later Borchardt endorsed this view.[3] It was over a decade later that Carter maintained they could not be Akhenaten and Nefertiti because they both wore king's crowns and they must be two male kings, shown as coregents. Newberry then published this theory in 1928[4] and it remained largely unquestioned until Harris upset it in 1973. He pointed out for the first time the evidence that the three cartouches on this stela would be for the two names of a king and one for a queen and would not represent a coregency which needs two for each king, as on the UC. stela (plate 55). He noted that Nefertiti did wear kings' crowns; that the embrace of the more feminine looking figure with an arm round the king was normal for Nefertiti when seated beside him; and that the neck of this figure had a concave curve where it joined the spine, an artistic con-vention usual for women at Amarna; while the neck of the other figure had the convex curve usual for men, and wore a king's pectoral. He recorded that so far there was no positive indication that Akhena-ten's successor was a man; and that Nefernefruaten, while still theore-tically queen, acquired the attributes of kingship. As noted above he posed the problem of "Two kingly persons of similar name, and not clearly distinguishable in any respect" . . "seen to succeed each other with no perceptible interval though without any overlap" and put the case for their identification, and for an objective re-assessment. He stated his evidence for the view that "Nefernefruaten/Smenkhkare was actually Nefertiti."

Following the first publication of this book in 1972, research continued on Amarna material in the Petrie Collection and was pre-pared for publication,[5] and evidence is accumulating that supports Harris's perception of Nefertiti's regality.

5. J. Samson, JEA 59. (1973) pp. 47-59; CdE XLVIII, 96 (1973) and L.101, (1976); JEA, 63 (1977).

VI RESEARCH AND DISCOVERIES IN THE 1970's

We are now in a better position to review the details of Amarna history as a whole than were earlier workers in the field. We have the material in the world's collections from excavations since Petrie's to compare with his, as well as the history which is being revealed from the building blocks (talatat) from the Aten temple at Karnak. From these it is evident that Nefertiti enacted a kingly role from the early years of the reign. On them we can see the Queen worshipping the god Aten without the intermediary of a king, in her own temple, alone or followed by her small daughter(s).

1. Nefertiti's Status

In a Preliminary Report Redford wrote that "Nefertiti shows a surprising degree of independence in the activities she performs"[1] and while she accompanies her husband in some of the offering and processional scenes, far more often she is depicted performing the offering alone in relation to the Aten. In his statistical presentation of the facts in Volume I of the Final Report, he shows that of "564 certain occurrences of the Queen's figure, crown or cartouches, only 14% show the King present by name or figure" (although "the actual percentage might have been slightly higher.").[2] On some temples named in the talatat "the Queen appears infrequently, and then in a role and position subordinate to that of the King; in others she seems to be the only royal figure present." This occurs in "so important a shrine as the Ḥwt-bnbn."[3] Redford writes "in spite of all possible explanations designed to rectify in the King's favour the numerical imbalance of occurrences the fact remains that Nefertiti had an

1. R. Redford JARCE 12(1975) p. 11

2. R. Redford ATP 1. (1976) p.80 N.32.
3. R. Redford op. cit. p. 81.

4. R. Redford *op. cit.* p. 82.

5. R. Redford *APT* 1: p. 82 pl.24; 25(1) 26 (2, 3) and end papers.

6. Davies. *Tomb of the Vizier Ramose* (1941) pl. XXXIII.
7. BM Stela 57.399
8. Hayes *Scepter of Egypt* (1968) Fig. 147.
9. Davies *RTA* 111 pls. IV; VIII and IX.

10. Davies, *RTA* IV, pl. XV; and Pendlebury *C/A* 111. pl. XXXI.

11. Wilson, *JNES* (1973) p. 239; (Sandman, *Texts from the time of Akhenaten*) (1938) p. 90.

importance in the *talatat* unsuspected hitherto. There is little doubt that this importance reflects a degree of power and influence incommensurate with her rank as Great King's Wife: she seems in this regard a true scion of the Eighteenth Dynasty's line of matriarchal Queens"[4]

It is now apparent that, while at Amarna Nefertiti is shown *beside* Akhenaten in palanquins, when worshipping, when enthroned, and when collaborating fully with him in state and religious affairs, in Thebes it is her independence that is stressed. This may have arisen from the need in Thebes to emphasise to the populace the revolutionary idea of a queen regnant with the king which, by the time of the move to Amarna, could have become an accepted fact. If the word spread around and from Thebes that Nefertiti worshipped the state god alone in her own temple, without the "divine" intervention of the King, the public would become aware of her regal and "divine" importance. In Thebes they could have seen her in the Jubilee Procession, carried in her own palanquin as the King was in his. They could have wondered at the phenomenon that, just as Akhenaten was surrounded by models of striding lions and male sphinxes and uraei, usual as King's emblems, Nefertiti has an array of "sphinxes surmounted by her head wearing the feathered crown"; and that the royal power signified by the raised head of a cobra ready to strike, was shown in friezes with "rows of rearing uraei with feminine profiles and coiffures" sometimes wearing tall feathers.[5] Such counterpart-symbols of kingship must have created something approaching awe in the people of Thebes as they recognised Nefertiti's status.

A queen shown as a natural size in a Window of Appearance beside the king and receiving the Ankh as Nefertiti is in the later scenes of the Theban tomb of Ramose, could be visualised as a royal partner.[6] Queen Ty was also emphasised as a recognisably royal person, possibly because as she was not of direct royal lineage, Amenhotep III thought it necessary to stress her status as Great Royal Wife. She too is shown a normal size and commemorated and portrayed beside her husband.[7] She is shown as a winged female sphinx holding his cartouche.[8] She retained her full queenly title at Amarna after his death, and is the only identifiable person there, other than Akhenaten and Nefertiti, to whose nose the Aten is shown presenting the breath of life.[9] *But,* she has not yet been found acting as a king in affairs of religion or state *in her own right.* She was queen with her husband and queen mother with her son. There is no scene of her in Theban or Amarna reliefs which suggests she is a regnant figure; none showing her holding the *sekhem* sceptre of authority as Nefertiti does where Akhenaten pours a libation on the altar.[10] Ty has not so far been found in scenes where she alone is in direct contact with the state god Amen, or Aten. But, Nefertiti is addressed by the word *dwȝ,* "praise", or "worship" or "adore" *which is normally connected with petitions to a god or king.* At Amarna she is addressed equally with Akhenaten and the Aten. Wilson wrote: "The hymns to the Aten begin with the worship of the Aten, of Akhenaten and of Nefertiti. No distinction is made among these three powers, except for the order in which they are named. All three are to be worshipped."[11]

122

In portraits of Nefertiti so far found she is shown as a feminine figure, mostly in a long gracefully pleated gown falling from her shoulders. She wears plain and ornate wigs; occasionally a king's crown; and very often, especially at Amarna, her uniquely shaped crown. As could be expected, however, when shown in the essentially traditional pose of Egyptian kings when they are about to vanquish foreign enemies, she wears more masculine attire. In the carving of this typically male scene on a block from Hermopolis she wears a topless belted kilt.[12] It resembles her dress on plate 21 above, where the ribs on the falling tie are visible. On the Hermopolis block Nefertiti, wearing her unmistakable crown, brandishes a ḫpš scimitar over the head of the captive whom she grasps by the hair. The ḫpš scimitar is clearly discernible in representations of the same kingly pursuit on a Theban block, where, worn though the surface is, Nefertiti is visibly wearing her distinctive crown and again, apparently, a topless, belted kilt. In the striding, traditionally conquering pose she faces the threatened captive. It is difficult to explain why Nefertiti should repeatedly be associated with this historically kingly iconography, for that is presumably all it is in this context, unless it was to portray her in a kingly role.

These significant manifestations of kingly status were carried through into small artistic details of the period. The Queen is shown on the right hand side of the King in statues and reliefs, instead of the more usual placing on the left; and she stands with one foot forward instead of the more usual feminine pose, of two feet together, see plate 5b. The Queen's own specific crown, always blue in the faience examples, is studded with discs: and she wears a King's cap-crown.[13] The Queen and her daughters are shown in painted statues and coloured inlays (see plates V and 45 ii) with the sun-tanned skin usual for men, instead of the pale, even yellow colour customarily chosen for women.

As could logically be expected, Nefertiti has nowhere been found carved, as queens are in some other reigns, knee-high to the King. Beside him she sits or stands in the proportionate size of a woman to a man, with her head nearly up to his shoulder, sometimes by or above it, although in the earlier sculptures carved in an exaggerated style Nefertiti's body is disproportionately short, just as parts of her body and the King's are disproportionately large, as on plate 20.

The iconographical instructions which were apparently issued to show Nefertiti as a regal partner of the King, equally participating in every sphere, were neither meaningless nor haphazard. It appears from later monuments as if the Queen's position became so accepted that it was rationalised by the artists who replaced earlier overstressing by more normal differentiations and naturalism.

(i) Queenly Ceremonies. As well as the Pase stela discussed above there is in Berlin another unfinished stela from Amarna with two un-named crowned figures on it.[1] One is a seated kingly figure who holds out a cup or goblet to a figure standing in front of him with the right arm raised to pour liquid from a small phial into the goblet.

12. Roeder, *Amarna-Reliefs aus Hermopolis;* p. 191; PC 67.
J. Cooney, *Amarna Reliefs from Hermopolis* (1965) Pl. 51a. J. Harris, *Acta Or.* XXXV(1973) p.9. and *Acta Or.* 36 (1974) n. 29.
R. Redford *ATP* 1. Pl.23(2).

13. E. Ertman *JARCE*, Vol. 13, 1976; pp. 63-67. Davies, *RTA*, 1, pl. XXX.

1. Staatliche Museum, Berlin No. 20716.

2. Schäfer, *Amtliche Berichte* 34; (1912-1913) 142. Borchardt *Porträts der Königin Nofret-ete* (1923) p. 9.

3. J. Harris *Acta. Or.* XXXV(1973) 7;
4. Davies *RTA* II (pl. XXXII).

5. I. Edwards BM *Treasures of Tutankhamen* (1972) No. 25. For similar vessels see Davies, *Tomb of Kenamun* pl. XX and *Nebamun and Ipuky* pl. XVII.
6. T. M. Davis, *The Tomb of Siptah* (1908) pp. 39/40, pls. IX; X.

1. Schäfer, *Amarna in Religion und Kunst* (1931) pl. 22.
2. I. Edwards, *Tutankhamen, his Tomb and Treasures* MMA. New York, (1976): endplates. (Facing this scene on the end-plates is the one from the shrine, of Tutankhamen pouring cooling drops(?) scent(?) into the hand of his Queen, from a phial of the shape used by the queens pouring into their husbands' "drinking vessels".

The figures were again recognised by Schäfer and Borchardt to be Akhenaten and Nefertiti.[2] But again, presumably for the same reason, because they both wore kings' crowns, controversy has ranged between the standing figure being Smenkhkare pouring wine for Akhenaten and Akhenaten pouring wine for his father. Harris has noted the parallel between this scene and that of Nefertiti pouring wine for Akhenaten in the tomb of Meryre II[3] These scenes, of a figure pouring a drink into a goblet held out by a king, appear to the writer possibly to have had a ceremonial significance and, as far as traced, the ceremony is performed by the "Great" queen. There were plenty of reliable court attendants to strain or pour the King's wine, but as recorded at Amarna it was Nefertiti who attended to it. Her pose in the tomb of Meryre II[4] is similar to that of the unnamed standing figure on the Berlin stela; and both pour the liquid into the out-stretched "cup" from the same type of small alabastron-shaped phial. Ankhesenamen assumes the same pose before the seated Tutankhamen as King, on his golden shrine with other ceremonial scenes on it. She is shown pouring the liquid from the same type of small phial into a large metal vessel resembling Akhenaten's goblet in Meryre's tomb but elaborately decorated. It appears to be twice as wide as the length of the King's hand that holds it. The small phial would hardly pour an adequate drink into this large vessel and the liquid apparently, would be unreachable over the high floral ornaments, which suggests it is a token offering with a particular meaning.[5]

In the Nineteenth Dynasty Queen Tawosret is shown on two wide silver bracelets standing in the same queenly pose before her seated husband Sety II. He holds a drinking goblet into which she is about to pour from a phial of the type used by the other queens.[6] While there is no evidence to substantiate the view that the standing figure on the Berlin stela is a man, there is comparative evidence which suggests that it is a queen and, as originally recognised by the excavators on the spot, that it is probably Nefertiti, wearing the *Khepresh* crown, in this queenly pose before her husband. Nefertiti's kingship and the crowns she wore did not preclude representations of her as "Great Wife", and mother.

(ii) Nefertiti centred under the Aten. Besides the criterion of the crowns, another detail has been mistakenly used for identifying unnamed, crowned Amarna figures. In the past, if a figure were centred under the disc beneath the straight or narrow-angled rays it was judged by some to be the King; if at the side of the picture, under the wider angled rays, the Queen. This often is the composition adopted, but not always. In one example on a fragment of another Berlin stela on which the only legible names are those of the Aten, Nefertiti, wearing her own distinctive crown, is centred under the rays.[1] She turns to the right towards the King, who is under the outer rays, to fasten his collar(?) or pectoral(?) while he waits with his arm resting apparently on the back of a chair or perhaps throne. There is a parallel scene on Tutankhamen's golden shrine.[2] On this the King and

Ankhesenamen are not beneath the Aten and they face in a reversed direction from her parents on the stela, but their relative position for the same procedure is the same. The King leans his left arm on the back of his seat while Ankhesenamen fastens his necklace; the hands of the two queens are in the same position to carry out this apparently queenly task which, like the pouring from the small phial and other scenes on this shrine, may have a ceremonial significance.[3]

In the nobles' tombs at Amarna, scenes showing Nefertiti centred under the Aten include those in which she drives her own chariot;[4] and where the King and Queen officiate side-by-side at the High Altar in the temple.[5] As would be expected, Nefertiti is in this central position where she is shown in reliefs in the kingly pose of smiting the enemy of Egypt with a $hp\check{s}$ scimitar.[6]

At the four corners of Akhenaten's sarcophagus from Amarna, where Nefertiti replaced the usual four goddesses, she is centred under the Aten's rays.[7] She is similarly placed under the rays on a fragment from Maketaten's sarcophagus.[8]

In volume I of Redford's publication of the Karnak blocks, Nefertiti is shown centred beneath the Aten on panels from the side of $Gm(t)$-$p\jmath$-itn gateway. In one scene she is officiating over the laden altar[9] and in another she lifts a stack of offerings to the centre.[10] This last block has been published recently with two very similar ones, labelled *Der König under der Strahlensonne*,[11] which demonstrates the need for a re-examination of royal scenes, and a re-thinking in the light of the present evidence of Nefertiti's status.

(iii) Nefertiti's names. As noted earlier the development of Nefertiti's names and titles and their links with Akhenaten's successor is fundamental to the study of the period and in the 1970's has been the subject of special research and study in depth.[1]

At Amarna the Queen's short name Nefertiti was quickly superseded by her long name Nefernefruaten-Nefertiti. On Boundary Stela K there is some evidence of when the change occurred. The *short* name is in the body of the text, as it could be expected in this, the earlier form of the dedication of the site. Davies wrote of the scene carved on the stela, that behind the King was his wife and daughter Meritaten, with the Queen's name Nefertiti above her and in front of her. He adds "This leaves no room for further figures; but the border has been erased and, a little space having been smoothed at the side, a tiny figure of Maketaten accompanied by an attendant, has been rudely inserted, and her name added in a column near her sisters."[2] He omitted, however, the fact that at the end of the inscription, in the last column, the Queen's *long* name appears, evidently also as a later addition at or about the time of the birth of Maketaten. Lepsius reproduced it[3] without comment, which it seems to have escaped until 1976.[4] From the Karnak Aten temple blocks Redford deduces that the addition of the Queen's Aten epithet (making her long name) "must have been made very early in the reign."[5]

Nefertiti's long name is remarkable for three things. In it the name of the god is written in reverse to face her queenly image, the signifi-

3. K. Bosse-Griffiths, *JEA* 59 (1973) p. 100ff.

4. Davies *RTA* 11 pl. XVI.
5. Davies *idem* pl. XVIII
6. R. Redford *ATP* 1 pl. 23(2): J. Cooney, *Amarna Reliefs from Hermopolis* (1965) pl. 51a.

7. G. Martin *The Royal Tomb at El-'Amarna 1.* pl. 19 (b) and (d), and 20(2).
8. Schäfer, *Amarna in Religion und Kunst* (1931) pl. 56.
9. R. Redford, *ATP* 1 (1976) pl. 19.
10. Redford *op. cit.* pl. 20(2)
11. *Nofretete, Echnaton,* Ägyptisches Museum Berlin (1976) pls. 18. 19. 20.

1. J. Harris *GM* 4. (1973) *Acta Or.* XXXV (1973) and 36 (1974). For Kiya, *CdE* XLIX; 97 (1974). Nims, *JNES* 32 (1973) p. 186 S. Tawfik *MDIK* 29(1) (1973) pp 82-86. Wilson *JNES* 32 (1973) p. 238. J. Samson *CdE* XLVIII; 96 (1973); and L. 101 (1976); *JEA*, 63 (1977).

2. Davies *RTA* V(1908) p. 25.
3. Lepsius *Denkmäler* Abb. 111 bl. 110 (b)
4. J. Samson *CdE* L; 101 (1976) p. 31. *(With thanks to Dr. G. Martin for confirming the presence of the long name, on his recent visit to the site).
5. R. Redford, *JARCE* XII (1975) p. 11.

cance of which was missed in earlier days (p. 112); secondly, this long name was repeated in two adjoining cartouches which resemble a king's two names; and thirdly, her Aten name is the early name of Akhenaten's coregent.

(iv) The Queen's double cartouche. The doubling of Nefertiti's long name in two cartouches has been explained above and is illustrated in plate 57, where the parallel with the two names of the King and the Aten is apparent. As noted, Queen Tawosret doubled her name similarly,[1] which gave her the equivalent of a king's nomen and prenomen, presumably before she adopted the name and titles of a king. Hayes wrote of her that "probably before the death of her husband" . . . "she, like Hatshepsut before her, discarded the title King's Great Wife and assumed the titulary of a reigning monarch."[2] The fact that Nefertiti also changed her wifely title has remained without comment for many years, but it is yet another link between her and the two queens, Hatshepsut and Tawosret, who ruled as kings.[3]

1. J. Harris, *Acta Or.* 36(1974) N.51.
2. Hayes, *Scepter of Egypt,* 2(1968) p. 357.
3. J. Samson, *CdE* L. 101 (1976) pp. 30-38.

(v) Nefertiti's wifely titles

In every description of Nefertiti so far traced by the writer she is described as Royal wife, or Great Royal Wife of the King in the usual form of *ḥmt nsw (wrt), except* in the tomb of Meryre II. In this, the only one that obviously spans the period between Akhenaten and his successor, she is described as *ḥmt nsw ꜥȝt.* The subtle difference between *wrt* and *ꜥȝt* is hard to assess; but the fact that the change of title occurs specifically over the names of the two *youngest* daughters points to it being a change that occurred in the later years at Amarna. The old formula for Nefertiti's description is clear over Maketaten and Ankhesenpaaten; the surface of the wall is broken away over Meritaten and damaged over the fourth daughter Nefernefruaten-the-younger. But over the two youngest princesses, Neferneferure and Setepenre, in whose names the Aten is replaced by Re, the Queen's new wifely title appears. It also occurs in the scene of Nefertiti straining the King's beverage into his out-stretched goblet, so presumably in his lifetime: and on an outer door jamb.[1]

In this tomb with such significant changes there is the unfinished drawing of two figures described by Davies as roughly sketched "the ink of which is now almost invisible", with many "false" lines and the figures restored on them "something of a travesty".[2] Had these figures been reliably visible they would probably have shown a picture of Akhenaten's successor: but as they are, they cannot. The now ghostly figures appear as though they were perhaps originally carved as Akhenaten and Nefertiti. Davies suggests the cartouches may also have been designed for Akhenaten and Nefertiti but that possibly the illness of the King, led eventually to the hasty execution of new cartouches.[3] Two of these contain the successor's names, King Ankhkheprure and Smenkhkare-djeserkhepru: and in the third, under *ḥmt nsw wrt,* (perhaps remaining from an original plan) is, not Meritaten, but *mry- ỉtn,* Beloved of the Aten. One of Nefertiti's titles was Beloved of the Living Aten.[4] In the past it has been suggested that

1. Davies, *RTA* II, pls. XXIX; XXXII; XXXVIII.
2. Davies, *op. cit.* p. 44 Note 2. pl. XLI.

3. Davies, *RTA* II. p. 44.
4. Davies, *RTA* V Pl. IV. (Redford *ATP,* "beloved of the living Disc") p. 82.

the figures represented a youth named Smenkhkare who was thought to have succeeded Akhenaten; and Meritaten who was thought to have married the youth. But so far there has been no identifiable representation of such a youth, and the cartouche beneath the queenly inscription does not read Meritaten because it is i) without the *.t* necessary in her name; ii) without the female figure usual in the princesses' names; and iii) without the determinative of a queen with a uraeus; whereas the full names of the successor have been accurately carved, and the epithet *mry-ỉtn* used here is used elsewhere by the successor. If by the death of Akhenaten, Nefertiti had been superseded by some other coregent, and successor, her face and figure and names would surely have been erased and replaced on his sarcophagus during the coregency. But they remain unaltered on the fragments, despite the destruction of the "heretic's" tomb furniture.

(vi) New evidence. Two pairs of cartouches on gold sequins, published by Harris in 1974, reveal the use by the successor of the epithet *mry-ỉtn*, Beloved of the Aten.[1]

In one (Fig. 15a) a *kingly* figure is allied to Nefertiti's Aten name, Nefernefruaten, with the reed in the name of the god Aten, reversed. This is only a partially retrograde writing of the gods name, but it was so turned for no one else except Nefertiti. Here, the reversed reed faces the kingly determinative which has the kingly attributes of the "king's beard", the flail and a *ḥkȝ* sceptre. There are many representations of this "king's beard", shown strapped on as part of the regalia. Hatshepsut is shown wearing one when she ruled. If this inscription were to be interpreted as the use of the name of Nefernefruaten by a youth as king, the unlikeliness of the regal adoption of the Queen's Aten name, apparently in her lifetime, must be faced. To cite but the one aspect of the contemporary scene already mentioned - at the death of Akhenaten his sarcophagus and everything else rescued from his despoiled tomb commemorate Nefertiti as the pre-eminent regal figure - save where she accompanies Akhenaten. Her portraits were not replaced during the coregency which surely would have occurred if anyone else had been the coregnant figure. In addition, it is doubtful if there had been such a king in this period from which literally innumerable named royal portraits survive, whether he could have been so undocumented that not one fragment of an authenticated portrait of him has been found anywhere. The cartouche on the other sequin of this pair (Fig. 15 b) reads Ankhkheprure-*mry-ỉtn*, (without a *.t*). Here, the phrase "Beloved of the Aten" in the same cartouche as the successor's prenomen, replaces the original epithet "Beloved of Akhenaten". It would be logical if this change occurred at the death of Akhenaten.

Of the other pair of inscribed gold sequins from the tomb of Tutankhamen, one contains the name Ankhkheprure (Fig. 16, b).[2] The other has the epithet *mry-ỉtn* - Beloved of the Aten - and a feminine determinative (Fig. 16a). This possibly replaced the function of the *.t* in the coregent's former epithet - Beloved of Akhenaten - i.e., to show it as feminine (Fig. 11). It would have been infinitely easier

1. . J. Harris *Acta Or.* 36(1974) pl. 17; Fig. 3. p.16.N.20, gold sequin, "apparently from the tomb of Tutankhamun" (Gunn *MSS* 1/14)"

a   b

Fig. 15

a   b

Fig. 16

2. J. Harris *Acta Or* 36 (1974) p.17 Fig. 2d (Carter obj. No. 45gg).

3. Davies *RTA* II, pl. XLI.

to inscribe a *.t* on this small fragile gold piece, rather than a female figure: but the *.t* would have turned the inscription into *Meritaten,* which was evidently not the aim. The difference can be appreciated if compared with her name spelt with a *.t* and followed by a determinative figure holding the lily(?), as in Figure 7, page 108. Without the female determinative, the phrase in Figure 16a resembles that used with the successor's names in the tomb of Meryre II[3] where, again the successor's names are correctly written, and the epithet is without the *.t.*

More examples may be found of the use by the successor of the epithet *mry-ỉtn,* Beloved-of-the-Aten. The phrase needs consideration which is disassociated from the former idea that it is evidence for the successor's marriage to Meritaten. Possibly there is a closer association with the fact that one of Nefertiti's titles was Beloved-of-the-Living-Aten (see p. 126). It must be remembered that neither at nor from Amarna, Thebes, Hermopolis, Memphis or elsewhere, is there one identifiable portrait of a young King named Smenkhkare, once thought to have married Meritaten. I am grateful to Professor Cambitoglou of Sydney University for the information that the only fragment from Memphis known there (Catalogued by Reeves in 1870) is the one with the names of Akhenaten and Nefertiti.

2.   *Meritaten's name and status*

Meritaten does not appear to have changed her name in any way. The impression is that, like Sitamen, she may have been outside the main stream of events and perhaps held some royal/religious office as princess royal. She is constantly described in connection with her father. At Maru Aten she is described as daughter of the King, not as Queen.[1] In the three places her name is mentioned in the extant Amarna Letters two relate to her father; the recipient of the third is not evident. Harris has now revealed that the former view that Nefertiti's name was erased in favour of her eldest daughter (always hard to believe) is not tenable in view of his finds on the material from Maru Aten and Hermopolis where it is Kiya's name that has been erased, not Nefertiti's.[2]

1. Gunn. *C/A.* 1.p.147 ff.
2. J Harris *CdE* XLIX, 97 (1974)
3. T. Davis, *Tomb of Iouiya and Touiyou* (1907), page 43 for Fig. 4.

Meritaten possibly stood in relation to her father as Sitamen did to Amenhotep III, to whom her title of King's Great Wife relates. Sitamen wore the uraeus and had her name in a cartouche, see plate 22. But there is ample evidence that although she was King's Great Wife, as Meritaten was, Sitamen in no way stepped into the role of her mother Queen Ty, nor in any way diminished her authority. She is pictured paying respects to Ty.[3]

Redford writes that in the early years at Karnak Meritaten appears everywhere as the eldest daughter. In the majority of scenes she is alone behind her mother, mainly where Nefertiti attends the Aten without the King. Exceptionally, Meritaten is also shown with her father. In one scene, alone behind her mother, a child is described by Redford as "what could be interpreted as *ḥmt-nsw, s3t-nsw n-ẖt-f*; King's-wife, King's-Daughter of his body."[4] He notes that "the bestowal on children of titles . . . perhaps in anticipation of their com-

4. R. Redford *ATP* 1.p.84.pl.19.

ing of age, is not unknown in ancient Egypt". At Amarna this same title is carved over the figure of the fourth daughter, Nefernefruaten, "the-younger", because she bears her mother's Aten name. This princess was born either just before the family left Thebes, or, much more probably, after the move to Amarna. The description is in the tomb of Meryre I,[5] with the later form of the Aten name i.e., after year 9. The princess stands in a chariot with her older sister Ankhesen-pa-aten who probably "holds the reigns". Nefernefruaten here would be little older than Meritaten was when holder of the title in Thebes, indicating the title was a royal honorific.

On two sections of an inscribed box (or boxes) from Tutankha-men's tomb Meritaten's name occurs in a cartouche with the title ḥmt nsw wrt, King's Great Wife. In one of the two inscriptions her name is shown with her father's name as King and his coregent's name as King Ankhkheprure - Beloved-of-Neferkheprure, Neferne-fruaten - Beloved-of-Waenre.[6] That these three people are named separately in one inscription demonstrates that it was not Meritaten who carried the successor's names and kingly title. But, with which King was she affiliated? (See fig. 7).

As a child in Thebes, she was called king's wife in relation to her father. Here she is called "King's Great Wife" as Sitamen was in re-lation to her father Amenhotep III. This was Nefertiti's title, which she is recorded as changing to ḥmt nsw ʿȝt from ḥmt nsw wrt late in the reign. It would be understandable if the description wrt were then given to Meritaten, especially if Nefertiti, like other queens known to have ruled as kings in ancient Egypt, eventually discarded her wifely title and adopted, if coregent, a new prenomen with her own Aten name Nefernefruaten and her own epithet, Beloved of Akhenaten.

In the second inscription on Tutankhamen's box,[7] Meritaten and the coregent are both described in the same way as in the first one which, again shows they were not one and the same person. But in view of the first inscription it cannot be taken as evidence that they were married. In neither inscription is Meritaten's determinative shown with a uraeus on her uncrowned wig.

(i) Names on Amarna blocks from Hermopolis. On the blocks from Amarna found at Hermopolis it is Akhenaten's name that occurs in relation to Meritaten-the-younger and Ankhesenpaaten-the-younger.[1] Had there been a young male king married to Meritaten his portrait or some reference to him could be expected to have been found in this context. But it has not been. It has been written that "The position of the king is still filled by Akhenaten (though nothing could prevent Smenkhkare as coregent from appearing in this role.)"[2] Noth-ing, that is, unless there were no male coregent. Nefertiti's long name appears repeatedly on the blocks.[3] This suggests they date to a period before the coregent's use of the name "Nefernefruaten", which would hardly be thus adopted, simultaneously with its occurrence in the name of the great Queen.[4]

It has been suggested that the Hermopolis blocks were "decorated

5. Davies *RTA* 1 pl. XIX.
6. J. Harris *Acta. Or.* 36 (1974) p. 13(1a).

7. J. Harris *Acta. Or.* 36 (1974) p.17 (2a, the strip).

1. Roeder *Amarna Reliefs aus Hermo-polis* (1969) *passim.*

2. Redford *ATP.* 1.p.93.

3. Roeder *Amarna Reliefs aus Hermo-polis* (1969), plates:- 1(137-111D); 2(137-111B); 3(245-VII); 29 (492 (VIII); 30(686-VIII); 106(451-VIIA); 163(869-VIII); and others; see Cooney *Reliefs from Hermopolis in American Collections* (1965) especially No. 17 p. 30.
4. Roeder *op. cit.* pl. 106 (451-VIIA).

129

5. R. Redford *ATP*. 1 p. 89.

6. R. Redford, *idem*.

7. Roeder *op. cit.* pl. 21 (454-VII): see *Ägyptisches Museum Catalogue* (1967) pl. 749; Inv. No. 14145.

8. Roeder, *op. cit.* plates 9(58-VIIIB); 12(485-VIIA) 172(PC 17) and others.
9. Harris *CdE.* XLIX.97 (1974) p.26 (Roeder, *op.cit.* pls. 20/21(454-VIIC) 22. (421-VII).
10. Roeder, *op. cit.* pl. 106 (831-VIIIe)
11. J. Harris, *CdE* XLIX.97 (1974) p.30,N.6. and pp.29/30.

1. R. Redford *ATP*. 1. p. 82.

at the close of Akhenaten's reign and/or during the reign of Smenkhkare" . . . "although his name is not found".[5] But in the writer's opinion there are indications that at least some of the blocks were earlier i.e., before the name Smenkhkare was used. These are i) the occurrence of Nefertiti's long name on them; ii) the absence of the name of the coregent with prenomen plus Nefernefruaten; iii) the absence of the name of the successor with prenomen plus Smenkhkare; iv) the style and proportion of some of the figures which resemble the earlier years rather than the later Amarna art. This particularly relates to three figures who occur as a trio of a king, queen (?) and small child. One suggestion is that this un-named trio might be Smenkhkare (the name has not been found on the blocks) with Meritaten and their daughter.[6] On the other hand, the king in the trio resembles the early rather caricatured representations of Akhenaten whose name so constantly appears on these blocks in relationship to Meritaten-the-younger and Ankhesenpaaten-the-younger. The kingly figure of the trio wears the bonnet-shaped Khepresh crown favoured by Akhenaten with, in one example, the clearly defined beaded edge which he wore when his and Nefertiti's daughters were young children, as on the Berlin stela (14145) with Nefertiti and the three eldest daughters and the early form of the Aten name, i.e.,[7] *before* c. year 9. By year 9 possibly five or even six of their daughters were born: but apparently no son. The lady who follows the king in the trio has no apparent uraeus on her bewigged but uncrowned head, and the wig is pushed back from her brow in the manner of some other portraits on these blocks.[8] Harris has noted that Kiya's name and the accompanying text appear on these blocks.[9] The king, therefore, followed by the uncrowned lady holding the hand of the small child could as easily be Akhenaten, Kiya and their child. Harris observes that Kiya was "Akhenaten's wife (ḥmt) over a period that would enable her to have been the mother of Tutankhaten" (whose name occurs on these Hermopolis blocks)[10] and, he continues "it is not improbable that it was she who in fact gave birth to the two younger daughters, Meritaten *tꜣ šrit* and Ankhesenpaaten *tꜣ šrit*."[11] Substantiated identification is not yet possible. But, if with more data this trio turned out to be Akhenaten, Kiya and their child, it would suggest that at least some of these blocks were from the middle years at Amarna when Akhenaten's virility is apparent from his growing family by Nefertiti. This could explain Akhenaten's paternity of a younger generation of royal daughters, on whose parentage we need more data, although they were brought into the family by being given the names of the first and third Amarna princesses, including "Aten" not yet replaced by "Re".

(ii) State Ownership. Meritaten's name has not been found as owner or part-owner of important, official state buildings or their equipment. On the other hand, Redford reports from Karnak that Nefertiti's name "is found frequently alone on offering tables as the (human) owner of the furniture, while Akhenaten is named on such tables only in conjunction with the Queen."[1] At Amarna Nefertiti's

name appears on the bricks of Panehesy's official house where her long name makes a kingly pair with Akhenaten's prenomen.[2] Pendlebury, in his two weeks preliminary excavation of the northernmost palace at Amarna, found that the largest proportion of the wine jars there were sealed with Nefertiti's name alone. The others were stamped *Hwt-itn*, House of the Aten. The scant reports of this part of the site already indicate Nefertiti's predominance in this area,[3] which probably holds the evidence needed for the history of the last years at Amarna.[4]

Bricks of the so-called coronation hall of the central palace which appears to be a subsequent addition to the building, are stamped with the name Smenkhkare, but the name of Meritaten has not appeared.[5]

There has been a learned and scholarly argument advanced in favour of Meritaten being her father's successor.[6] But in the present writer's opinion the inscriptions and monuments found at and from Amarna do not, so far, bear this out. The fact that Meritaten appears in the same inscription as her father, *and his successor* as King Ankhkheprure-Nefernefruaten, argues pointedly against these names belonging to Meritaten. As noted there is as yet no authentic evidence of a marriage between Meritaten and a male successor, or of the existence of such a successor.

3. Queens who ruled in ancient Egypt

Procedures adopted by Akhenaten's coregent and successor which are similar to those of the three queens known to have ruled as kings, include the following parallels. Some are noted elsewhere.

The doubling of Nefertiti's long name in two adjacent cartouches resembling a kingly prenomen and nomen, was also used by Queen Tawosret[1] (see p. 111)

The adoption by the coregent of a feminine .*t* in the prenomen (p. 113) is an echo of Hatshepsut's measure of adding it to the word "king" to make it a feminine noun.[2]

Hatshepsut and Tawosret both discarded their wifely titles, the latter "probably before the death of her husband".[3] Nefertiti changed hers and the late variation is found in a position which places it in Akhenaten's lifetime: (p. 126).[4]

Before the adoption of the name Smenkhkare, as Harris has pointed out, the name-change matched the form of the three other queens who ruled as sole kings, in that all adopted a new prenomen and used their queenly name plus an epithet as their nomen. The reason for the new nomen is discussed on p. 132. (See table overleaf).

Akhenaten's coregent (like Hatshepsut and Tawosret) adopted the title "Son of Re", usual in king's titles. An example of this is in the Theban tomb of one Pere, at the beginning of a petition to the god Amen.[5] The inscription has previously been accepted as indicating that Smenkhkare (the name is not mentioned) a male successor to Akhenaten returned to Thebes, to the worship of Amen, and for burial.[6] But Pere was a priest of Amen and could hardly omit the god from his mortuary chapel. Nevertheless, he begins his petition with the date (year 3) and addresses the coregent as King Ankhkheprure-

2. Pendlebury, *C/A*. III.
1. page 26; and 2. plate LXXXIII.
3. Whittemore *JEA* 12(1926); Pendlebury *JEA* 17 (1931): *JEA* 18 (1932) p. 144.
4. J. Samson *CdE* XLVIII; 96(1973).
5. Pendlebury *C/A* III pt.1. pp. 60 and 80.
6. R. Krauss. *Hildesheimer, Ägyptologische Beitrage* Vol. 6. Forthcoming.

1. Vernier, *Bijoux et Orfèvreries; CCG.* (1907) 97. Nos. 52264-65.
2. Naville, *Temple of Deir el Bahari* (1894) p.16, *Passim.*
3. Hayes, *Scepter of Egypt*, 2; (1968) p. 357.
4. Davies *RTA* 11 pls. XXIX; XXXII; and XXXVIII.

5. Gardiner *JEA* 14 (1928) pp.10-11
6. C. Aldred *CAH* Vol. II, XIX (IV) (1971) p. 17.

Prenomen	Personal name with royal nomen
Nefrusobk/ Sebeknofru (12th Dynasty)	became Sebekkare': Nefrusebk/ Sebeknofru
Hatshepsut (Earlier 18th Dynasty)	became Makare': Hatshepsut-Meryetamun
Nefernefruaten Nefertiti (Later 18th Dynasty)	Ankhkeprure mry Akhenaten: *Nefernefruaten mry Akhenaten. * later, Smenkhkare-djeser-khepru.
Tawosret (19th Dynasty)	became Sitre'-meryetamun: Tawosret-Sebekenmut

Table: *Queens who ruled in Ancient Egypt.*

Beloved-of-Akhenaten, Nefernefruaten - Beloved-of-Akhenaten. Akhenaten *per se* is not addressed here. The date "Year 3" may be found to relate to the official coregency.

The title "Son of Re", which occurs in its usual place in the titles of the coregent in this inscription, can no longer be attributed only to male rulers. It is in the titulary of Tawosret on two limestone bricks from her mortuary temple in the Valley of the Kings;[7] and was used repeatedly by Hatshepsut, although not to the exclusion of "Daughter of Re".[8]

4.   The use of the new names Nefernefruaten and Smenkhkare

The name Smenkhkare has frequently been used in relation to inscriptions in which it does not appear. This has possibly blurred a time element between the coregent's apparent use of the name Ankhkheprure; Nefernefruaten; and the apparently later use of Ankhkheprure; Smenkhkare-djeserkhepru.

The coregent's prenomen Ankhkheprure, sometimes spelt with a feminine .t (pl. 58), is customarily linked to Akhenaten with the epithet Beloved of "Neferkheprure," (Akhenaten's prenomen) or "Waenre" (his epithet): Harris has now recorded the use of the nomen Akhenaten, with Nefernefruaten, in a palimpsest inscription on a pectoral from Tutankhamen's tomb;[1] another example is on the coregency stela plate 55a; and a third has recently been traced, on a ring bezel in the Metropolitan Museum New York, as at Fig. 17.[2] But none of these epithets linked to Akhenaten, nor the use of the feminine .t, nor the use of the name Nefernefruaten, has been found with the coregent's prenomen Ankhkheprure *when this is combined with the new nomen,* or throne name, Smenkhkare.

Of the nomen Smenkhkare, Harris has written "Not only was it the latest (and final) variant of the nomen, as intimated by Petrie and recently stated again",[3] but with the accompanying variants of the prenomen, it is less common than forms of the earlier name Ankhkheprure mry X; Nefernefruaten mry Y. He also notes: "the evidence is that the epithets naming Akhenaten were not in use after his death and this is in all probability linked with Amarna concepts of kingship and death and with the altered 'mortuary' status of the prenomen and nomen."[4]

7. Hayes, *Scepter of Egypt* (1968) p. 358.
8. Hayes, *op. cit.* pp. 82-105.

Fig. 17

1. J. Harris *CdE* XLVIII 96(1973) postscript p. 250.
2. MMA.No.10.130-947 with thanks to the Department of Egyptian Art for the information.
3. J. Harris *Acta.Or.* XXXV (1973) N.5. and P.*T/A* p.29. Also Munro *ZÄS* XCV (1969) 113-115; H.-W. Helck *CdE* XLIV (1969) pp.206-7.
4. J. Harris *op.cit.* 36(1974)N.14.

The use of Smenkhkare as a throne name by Akhenaten's successor has great relevance to the last years at Amarna. From the original policy of including "Aten" in the names of the King, Queen and four eldest daughters, came the change in the names of the two youngest daughters to include "Re" instead of the Aten. The fifth princess is Nefernefrure, her mother's Aten name with the Aten changed to Re; the youngest is Setepenre.

The fourth daughter who had her mother's Aten name, Nefernefruaten (the younger), was born some years after her mother adopted it. As noted, the child was later entitled King's Wife, King's Daughter beloved of him, as Meritaten was at Karnak (p. 129). When considered in its context it does not seem compatible with the significance of a person's name in ancient Egypt that this name would be used a third time at Amarna for a youth whom Akhenaten was thought to have made his coregent. Neither would it appear suitable, being the name of one of the princesses, for the successor to have used it as a throne name. It could not have been changed to Nefernefrure because that was the name of the fifth princess. So a new throne name was imperative, hence Smenkhkare.

The incorporation of the "ka" of Re in the name, as Smith has pointed out to us, is reminiscent of earlier centuries. Queen Sebek-Ka-Re who ruled in the twelfth dynasty, and Queen Hatshepsut, (Maat-ka-re), ruling earlier in the eighteenth dynasty, both incorporated it; Tawosret was Sitre. The adoption of Re in the names of the youngest daughters was clearly more acceptable to Akhenaten than the more radical change by Tutankhaten to -amen, and the third princess from Ankhesenpaaten, to Ankhesenamen.

5. Evidence of Nefertiti's kingship

(i) Regalia. The task of representing Akhenaten and Nefertiti as equals was facilitated by their occasional adoption of similar types of wigs and crowns and clothing. Both wore the "bag" or Afnet wig with uraeus, as the Queen does on plate 20. Nefertiti wore the Atef crown[1] and the Red *dšrt* crown as Kings'[2] did. As noted elsewhere there are a number of instances suggesting she wore the Blue, Khepresh crown, viz., on the two unfinished stelae in Berlin (page 123); and in the double outline of the figures of the King and Queen in the tribute scene of the tomb of Meryre II where this can be inferred.[3] A relief on Akhenaten's sarcophagus suggests that she may be wearing the Khepresh crown, but it is very damaged;[4] the curved front line of the tall crown she wears does not resemble her own straight-sided head-dress, while the straight line remaining at the back does not appear to be her cap crown. What remains of the front section could possibly have been decorated with discs as well as the uraeus. For Nefertiti's crowns to have been studded with discs, which is the traditional pattern for the Khepresh crown, was an innovation and in itself a means of emphasising similarity. The discs are convincingly shown on her stone crown in Cairo as well as on the faience

1. Davies *RTA* II, pl. VIII.
2. Davies *RTA* III p. 10. See also Harris, *Acta Or.* XXXV(1973) pp 9-13.
3. Davies *RTA* II pl. XXXVIII.
4. G. Martin, *The Royal Tomb at El Amarna* (1974) pl.21.

examples from Amarna in the Collection (pp. 115-8).

Akhenaten, like Nefertiti, wore her distinctive blue crown topped by the disc, rams horns and plumes.[5] He wore long gowns as she did, but apparently to his ankles whereas hers reached the ground. The attributes of kingship shared by the King and the Queen were suitably adapted. The Queen's Atef crown is smaller and minus the hawks, which are also omitted from Tutankhamen's version on the back of his golden throne. (Pl 14b.)[6] The Queen's straight-sided blue crown has a neater line than the rather bulging Khepresh crown, worn by Akhenaten and possibly by Nefertiti too when occasion demanded it. His gowns were shorter and less feminine than hers.[7] There is a suggestion of elegance in the adaptation of the regalia.

(ii) Activities. In the carved reliefs at Amarna every opportunity seems to have been taken to convey the Queen's status.[1] Examples imply a joint reign resembling that of William and Mary in 17th century England. In official scenes at Amarna, when the King and Queen are seated, the Queen is mostly shown sitting beside the King. In the tribute scene of the tomb of Meryre II Nefertiti sits on the far side of the King who holds her by the hand. Her feet, legs and shoulder with part of a streamer from her crown are shown in outline behind him, but her crown is completely obliterated as though it is the same Khepresh shape.[2] Harris has commented on the exceptional drafting of two major figures with a duplicate outline here, and in two other scenes where the same crown might be assumed.[3] One is where the King and Queen are standing in front of the Great Altar[4] and the other where they are carried shoulder high in the state palanquin.[5] In the last scene Davies has outlined the Red (*dšrt*) crowns they wear in a drawing showing the Queen's profile and the flail she carries.

A less formal scene at the door of the palace is an example of the conceptual imagery in Egyptian art. The King and Queen are seated on chairs with the royal emblems of Upper and Lower Egypt.[6] But she is shown *behind* him. The head and torso of the Queen have been carefully cut from the wall, doubtless by tomb robbers, but it is still clear that she had one of the children on her knee whom she held with her right hand.

(iii) Public appearances. In Windows of Appearance at Amarna Nefertiti apparently helped the King to dispense royal honours. She appears to have handed a gold collar over the edge of the Window to Huya;[1] and two in another scene for Ay[2] with Meritaten and Maketaten helping their parents, possibly as a means of keeping them happy and teaching them royal duties. Ankhesenpaaten seems too young for this and is in the crook of her mother's left arm as she strokes her mother on the chin.

5. Pendlebury *C/A III* (1951) LXIX (4); C. Aldred, *Akhenaten and Nefertiti* (1973) Fig. 31; No. 31. J. Samson, *JEA*, 63 (1977) Fig. 2.
6. C. Desroches Noblecourt, *Tutankhamen* (1963) pl. VI.
7. Davies, *RTA* (II; pl. VIII) *passim.*

1. Davies *RTA.* passim. * So many relevant scenes in these next pages are in the six volumes on *The Rock Tombs of El Amarna*, produced by N. de Garis Davies for the EES (Fund) 1903-1908 that most references are simply *RTA*, with number of volume, plate and/or page.
2. Davies *RTA* II; XXXVII-VIII.
3. J. Harris *Acta Or.* XXXV (1973) pp. 11-12.
4. Davies *RTA* II; XVIII.
5. *RTA* III; XIII. p. 10.
6. *RTA* VI; XVII.

1. Davies *RTA* III; XVII.
2. *RTA* VI; XXIX.

In chariot scenes the Queen sometimes drives her own chariot in kingly style,[3] equipped with a sheathed bow and arrows, although in this reign the King does not appear to have been given to shooting his enemies or hunting game. In the tombs of Mahu and Ahmes,[4] the King and Queen face each other in the same chariot which is driven by the King and, centred under the Aten's rays they even share as equals the one Ankh held in the god's hand. The princesses are also equipped with the likeness of the bows and arrows (toys?), in their smaller chariots which they drive,[5] perhaps to teach them to manage horses as both their parents are shown doing.

3. *RTA* II; XVL
4. *RTA* IV; XX. III; XXXIIA.
5. *RTA* II; XV

(iv) Family Life. Numerous facets of the family life shared by Akhenaten and Nefertiti with their children, and with Queen Ty on her visit to Amarna, are recorded as natural occurrences.[1] To discredit the genuineness of these scenes of a united family, and those so movingly portrayed of the grief of the King and Queen at the death of their second daughter,[2] supposes a degree of cynical deviousness that is nowhere apparent or suggested in any of the multitudinous scenes of the period. Even the monkey statuettes (humorous toys?) which some have suggested are an echo of royal life, show parental affection above all, as well as the playfulness of the young (plates 16 and 17).

1. *RTA* III; VI.
2. Bouriant, Legrain, *Monuments du Culte d'Atonou en Egypte* Vol. 1 (1903).

(v) Scenes of worship. From the early period at Amarna when the scenes were carved on the Boundary Stelae, the King and Queen are repeatedly shown worshipping the Aten together, carved thus in reliefs in the rock tombs, and on the walls, stelae, balustrades, doors and lintels of state buildings, and in private homes. In them all Akhenaten and Nefertiti stand equally under the god. The King is usually shown beside the laden altars with Nefertiti behind him (sic) although clearly she sometimes stood beside him, as is actually shown at the altar of the Great Temple.[1] But they are often shown enacting different rituals which could not be specified if one figure were beyond the other. Sometimes they stand on opposite sides of the altar.

1. . Davies *RTA* II; XVIII.

At the Great Temple altar, as noted above, they stand beside each other beneath their three cartouches as Lord and Lady of the Two Lands. This is not a picture of a queen-goddess conferring the benefits of a cult on the King; this is two equally royal and "divine" rulers standing in the same relationship to the god they worship.

In reliefs where the Queen is shown under the outer rays of the Aten, the hands on the ends of the sun's rays reach down equally to the King and Queen. There can be no doubt about her total inclusion in its blessings. The god presents the Ankh, the breath of life, only to her nose and the King's; a hand blesses her offering, the uraeus on her crown and sometimes stretches to the back of her head and/or holds her arm as if to draw her into its ambience.

In a scene of elaborate iconography in the tomb of Apy,[2] Nefertiti, behind the King, has a separate altar in front of her. This the Aten blesses, while holding her elbow and stretching out a hand to

2. Davies *RTA* IV, XXXI.

3. P.*T/A* Pl. XII (1 and 2).

bless her offering and her crown. Both the King and Queen offer plaques bearing the Aten's two names mounted on tables. The King's pair of plaques are flanked on both sides with standing figures of the god Shu with arms up-raised to the Aten names. On the Queen's offering table it is her own squatting figure who "adores" the Aten with arms upraised. The linked iconography of the squatting worshipping figure, the sun god, and Shu, is known in other instances. One is on fragments of a stela found by Petrie.[3] On this the King and Queen are both shown on both sides of the altar. Unfortunately the King's offering and much of his figure are broken away. On the left the Queen offers the Aten names on a *nb* sign. On the right she offers a *nb* sign on which her own image wearing the feathers of Shu is squatting, and offering the Aten names flanked on one side by *Ankh* and *Djed* signs and on the other by a *W3s* sign. Both she, and the King in front of her, raise their left arms in adoration.

Harris has studied this iconography and recently published a faience nob from a private Danish collection which has parallels. On this there are two solar barks. At one end of each bark is a squatting royal figure with arms upraised in adoration of a plain solar disc at the other end. The figure under the name Akhenaten wears a kingly white crown; the other, under the name Nefertiti, "wears the characteristic flat-topped cap associated with Nefertiti". Harris notes the emphasis on the similar formal status of the royal figures "equated in size, in symbolism of stance and gesture, and their relationship to the sun disc. The manner in which they are paired", he writes "suggests indeed that they are assimilated to Shu and Tefenet."[4] He points out that at various levels "the form of the representation alludes to the solar nature of the royal couple, and to their virtual parity in the particular context. The extent to which Nefertiti was seen as the counterpart of Akhenaten, and acknowledged as such, whether in terms of her theological status or ultimately as ruler, has lately become the centre of much discussion. Few items of evidence are as explicit as this in an iconographical sense, and the piece is thus of considerable relevance as a historical document".

4. J. Harris, *Burlington Magazine* CXIX (89) (May 1977) pp.340-343; Figs. 33 - 39.

In some of the Amarna scenes of worship the King and Queen practise the same rituals; in others different ones. Sometimes both offer fragrant gifts or libations on one side of the altar and are shown censing the Aten on the other.[5] Sometimes both offer loaves of bread;[6] or one offers a libation and the other carries flames in a bowl.[7] In some of the carvings they both pray or worship with upraised arms as they do on Boundary Stela N.[8] In some scenes they both offer the *Sekhem* Sceptre of authority;[9] sometimes only Nefertiti holds this symbol of power, as in the tomb of Mahu.[10] The ceremonial duties of Akhenaten and Nefertiti at Amarna are shown to be equal in so many different ways and variations as to indicate a consciously recorded iconography. Nefertiti clearly held a kingly position in relation to the state god Aten in her husband's lifetime and her participation with him is thus carved.

5. Davies *RTA* II; V.
6. *RTA* IV; XXIII.
7. *RTA*, VI, XVI.
8. *RTA* V; XXXVII.
9. *RTA* I; XXV/XXVII;
10. *RTA* IV; XV

In the Amarna texts prayers are addressed by the owners of the tombs to the powers who might confer benefits upon them. The hymns or petitions are offered equally to the King and Queen or to the Aten, King and Queen. "The petitions are interchangeable; the Queen may be asked for the same benefits as the god or King."[11] A clearer evidence of kingship does not exist; and among Egyptian Pharaohs only Akhenaten and Nefertiti share it.

11. Wilson, *JNES* (1973) p. 239 (Sandman, *The Time of Akhenaten* (1938) pp.17-20; 26-7.) Davies *RTA* I p.52(4) ff.

CONCLUSIONS

What emerges clearly and unquestionably in studying the facts of Nefertiti's kingship is that no data has been found for any figure of comparable kingly status in this period except Akhenaten. As Harris has seen, with the evidence of Nefertiti's regality it is difficult to envisage how there could have been another undistinguishable, contemporary regnant figure.

In the early days of the reign in Thebes, Nefertiti's status was already kingly. She owned temple furniture. She had her own temple, and in it and in other temples she worshipped and attended on the state god without the intermediary of the "divinity" of a king, which does not suggest the status of a queen. She was carried in the *ḥb-sd* procession surrounded by the same symbols of royal power as the King, but shown unmistakably in her own image. She is pictured vanquishing the enemies of Egypt in specifically kingly iconography.

At Amarna her status is defined less dramatically but in even more detail. The thinking behind the exposition of her status is evident in many scenes of every day life in the city. Omitting such details as her stance and personal presentation, she is pictured as sharing every aspect of religious, court and state officialdom with her husband. She awards honours, is carried shoulder-high with him, attends levees, all of which, although unusual, could be claimed as possible occasions for a queen. But it is in kingly fashion that she wears regalia, smites the foe, drives her own chariot, and not only attends the god with the King but officiates equally with him at the altars. She is addressed by the word *dwꜣ* as "praise", "worship"; a form of reverent address which is normally confined to a god or king; and she is petitioned equally with the god and the King for "divine" benefits. All these facts are carved in stone.

Significant changes are recorded in the Queen's names and title during the course of the reign. In Thebes came the introduction of Nefertiti's long name and in it the phenomenon of the god's name being written backwards to face her image. In the later years, with a new prenomen it is Nefertiti's Aten name and her own epithet that constitute the name of Akhenaten's coregent. This form of nomenclature of the coregent is a parallel with that of the three queens who are known to have ruled Egypt as kings. Considered in its context, the idea that the Queen's Aten name and her epithet were passed on to a youth set on the throne of Egypt by Akhenaten does not appear compatible either with the dignity of names or the custom in ancient Egypt: it is certainly at variance with the fact that the prenomen has

137

now been recognised to have been written at times as a feminine name: and the fact that no identifiable portrait of a kingly youth has been found, only portraits of the Queen with kingly attributes.

On the Hermopolis blocks from Amarna Akhenaten is the only king named in relation to the younger generation of royal children, Meritaten-the-younger and Ankhesenpaaten-the-younger. But Nefertiti's long name occurs on these blocks and it is improbable that the name Nefernefruaten would be used simultaneously in her name and in a coregent's name.

The suggestion that the eldest daughter Meritaten used her mother's Aten name and succeeded Akhenaten is not supported by evidence from Amarna. She and at least one of her younger sisters, when small children, as well as being entitled "King's Daughter" were called "King's Wife", which can reasonably be accepted as an honorific. Later, Meritaten, the eldest daughter, became "King's Great Wife", as Sitamen did to her father Amenhotep III in the previous reign. But Sitamen has not been found anywhere recorded as a ruler of Egypt; nor as an equal to her mother, the "King's Great Wife" Queen Ty, to whom she is shown paying respects. The former belief that Nefertiti's name was over-carved by Meritaten's in a number of places has been dispelled by the discovery that it was Kiya's name that was thus overcarved. Nefertiti changed the form of her wifely title in the later years of the reign at Amarna and may, like the queens known to have ruled as kings, have eventually abandoned it. In any case, the appearance of Meritaten's name, entitled "King's Great Wife" in an inscription with both her father's name and his coregent, both described as Kings, makes it possible that she held her title in relation to her father, but impossible for her to have been the other King - Ankhkheprure-Nefernefruaten.

As the phrase *mry-itn*, Beloved of the Aten, has now been found used as an epithet in the successor's name, in one instance in the same cartouche, it has now to be disassociated from a former idea that it proved *Meritaten* was married to the successor. No scene or description relating to such a marriage has been found and the only name on the bricks of the so-called coronation hall of the central palace is Smenkhkare.

A number of Egyptologists in different countries are studying Amarna material for evidence of the history of the period in which there are still gaps to be filled. Signposts which have been overlooked in the past are being recognised. Doubtless more data and knowledge will accrue from further research and excavations, at Karnak, and when possible at the northernmost palace at Amarna, where on present evidence, scant though it is, Nefertiti appears to have been paramount and where, on the ceremonial gateway, her name did not appear - unless it was as Smenkhkare.

Finally, on known monuments from Akhenaten's lifetime only Nefertiti is recorded with the attributes of a co-ruler. Had she died before Akhenaten or been superseded by the time he died it could be expected that her portraits on his sarcophagus, where she is shown beneath the Aten as sole and supreme authority, would have been replaced during the coregency of some other ruler. But they were not. On the fragments of the "heretic's" funeral furniture, Nefertiti's face and figure are recognisably unaltered. The logical sequence would then be that the Queen succeeded her husband as Pharaoh until the accession of the young Tutankhaten-amen and her daughter, in about 1350 B.C.

GENERAL INDEX